Basics Of Ethical Hacking: A Comprehensive Beginners Guide

SADANAND PUJARI

Published by SADANAND PUJARI, 2024.

Table of Contents

Copyright 1

About 2

Introduction 3

Cybersecurity 8

Current Cybersecurity Market 10

The 3 Types of Hackers 15

The 4 Elements of Security 18

Ethical Hacker Terminology 21

Common Methods of Hacking 23

Cybersecurity & Ethical Hacking Overview 28

Ethical Hacking vs Penetration Testing 30

Job Opportunities in Cybersecurity 34

Networking chapter Overview 35

How Data Travels Across The Internet 42

Understanding Ports and Protocols 44

Understanding IP Addresses: Public & Private 49

What Are Subnets? 51

The Average Network vs Remote Based 53

- Hacking Lab chapter Overview 57
- Understanding Virtual Machines 62
- Setup Your Kali Linux Machine 64
- VN Setup & Testing Vulnerable Systems 69
- Linux+Python+Bash+Powershell chapter Overview 81
- Linux Basics 85
- Working With Directories & Moving Files 91
- Installing & Updating Application Files 93
- Linux Text Editors 95
- Searching For Files 98
- Bash Scripting Basics 100
- Python Basics 105
- Remaining Anonymous chapter Overview 111
- TOR Browser Overview 115
- Anonsurf Overview 118
- Changing Mac Addresses 120
- Using a Virtual Private Network/Server (VPN, VPS) 122
- WiFi Hacking chapter Overview 125
- WiFi Hacking System Setup 129

WEP Hacking Attack #1..134

WEP Hacking Attack #2..139

What Next..142

Copyright

Copyright © 2024 by **SADANAND PUJARI**

All rights reserved. No part of this book may be reproduced, scanned, or distributed in any printed or electronic form without permission. Please do not participate in or encourage piracy of copyrighted materials in violation of the author's rights. Purchase only authorized editions.

Basics Of Ethical Hacking: A Comprehensive Beginners Guide

Unlock The World Of Cybersecurity Learn The Fundamentals Of Ethical Hacking Today!

First Edition: Jun 2024

Book Design by **SADANAND PUJARI**

About

This Book is comprehensive, showing you both sides of hacking. You will learn to think and operate like a hacker – and how to apply that knowledge as a cybersecurity expert to protect you and your clients' networks and systems. In taking this 'cat and mouse' approach, your rounded understanding will give your approach new depths and angles, revealing the paths you can take to effectively neutralize any threat.

Together with the emphasis on practical examples that you can follow in real life with live systems, you will also benefit from the excitement of hands-on learning. By experiencing precisely what it takes to hack into any given target system, you'll also learn that no one system is the same and that all approaches can be modified.

This real-life learning is an invaluable part of your education, enabling you to better see what hackers are doing and how to block even the most potent attacks. No matter what the scenario or how complicated a hacking situation, this Book gives you the foundational training you need to secure a network – and start pursuing a career in a field that is increasingly in demand as the global reliance on technology grows.

Introduction

Welcome to the Book. In this chapter, we're going to go over the exact Book content that we're going to go over in this entire beginning to expert ethical hacking Book. We're going to go over each particular chapter. We're going to cover the different data points that we're going to cover within each chapter. And I want you to really have this big picture overview so you can kind of get an idea as far as what's in store for this entire Book is going to essentially give you that big picture, macro perspective, 50000 foot view. So you have the eagle eye's view of what exactly we're going to cover and what we're going to go very much so in depth. Now, the way that this Book is going to be structured is I myself am going to be primarily focusing on the core chapter overviews. I'm going to be the one that's starting out each particular chapter, giving the big picture overview.

And then Anthony is going to be the one that's going into the actual individual chapters, showing you exactly how to go about the different lessons, the different material and the different tips and techniques that are going to be taught within this Book. So I just wanted to go ahead and give you an overview of how this is going to be. Now, one other thing to keep in mind here is that at the end of each chapter, there's going to be a list of questions, anywhere between three to five. Sometimes you may have more. And so those are going to help you get a better understanding and kind of a review after each chapter. So make sure that you go through those as well, because you're going to help you make sure that that information stays top of mind and it's going to help you make sure that this information gets solidified while you're going through each particular chapter. So let's go right ahead and jump into the chapters on what exactly we're going to cover here.

And so here are the chapters, one through seven in the Book introduction chapter one. We're going to go over the three types of hackers. We're going to go over the four elements of security. We're going to go over some important terminology for ethical hackers. chapter two, this is where we're going to go over the network basics. We're going to show you exactly what a network is, how the data travels across the web and understanding the ports and protocols and how they are involved within the networking chapter. And then chapter three, we're going to go over how to set up your hacking lab, understanding virtual machines, virtualization, how to install CALEIGH Linux into your virtual server there into your virtual machine, and then finding vulnerable systems to actually test. And then chapter four, we're going to go over the Linux Python bash and power show basics. We're going to cover the basics of Linux, working with directories and then the Basche in Python scripting basics.

Very important for you to understand both of these here and especially Python, as it's one of the most popular scripting languages within the ethical hacker community. And then chapter five, how to remain anonymous on the Web. We're going to go over the Tor browser overview, how to change your Mac address and then using virtual private networks, VPN and the importance of these when you're actually doing ethical hacking and to help you with becoming very much so anonymous so that none of your tracks are actually being found out. Right. You're covering your tracks and you're remaining as anonymous as possible. And then number six, we're going to go over how to hack wifi. We're going to go over WSP hacking, WPA and WPA hacking. And then chapter seven, we're going to go over the passive and active reconnaissance, essentially information gathering. We're going to go over the differences between passive and active recon.

We're going to go over Google hacking. And then in chapter eight, we're going to go over launching attacks. We're going to cover how to search for exploits, create custom payloads and then how to avoid being detected by an antivirus. So make sure that when you are aware that there is an actual antivirus there, how you can maneuver and go around through different loopholes so you're not being detected. Right. And then chapter nine post exploitation, we're going to go over privileged escalation, installing a back door and then finding cache credentials. And then chapter 10, we're going to go over website and application hacking, how to find and gather the target information for a particular website or a particular application. We're going to go over the website scanning our Web application scanning as well. And then chapter 11, we're going to.

Over mobile phone security and hacking, we're going to go over what exactly are mobile attack vectors and we're going to go over mobile malware and how that comes into play and how you can stay protected and then mobile hacking using your LS. And also within that chapter, you're going to learn how you can stay protected against different types of hackers that are, you know, trying to get your information, try to get a hold of your cell phone. So that's going to be a very exciting chapter as well. And then chapter 12, we're going to go into getting your name out there. As an ethical hacker, how can you separate yourself from the competition? Get your name out there and essentially make yourself one of the top hackers in your actual niche or in your market. So we're going to cover building a brand, writing a book and networking.

So those three are probably one of the most important things that you can do for your career. And as far as the building, a brand that's going to be more centered around if you want to build the company or if you want to do the personal branding where you are essentially the brand and then writing a book, I mean, that's very, very simple, especially nowadays, where you can create a book on Amazon Kindle, publish it through self publishing and automatically be able to differentiate yourself in the marketplace and get that instant credibility and authority. And then networking, like I mentioned, this is something that is crucial also for your career, being able to leverage your relationships, your connections, but then also be able to build new ones, but then going about it the right way where you're not just going at the actual networking with your pure self interest. OK, so we're going to talk about some of the dos and don'ts and networking.

And then chapter 13, we're going to go over how to make money as a hacker. We're going to go over the bug bunny programs, what exactly those are and how you can make money with those. And then we're going to go over freelancing. What exactly is involved with that? How you can start freelancing right away and then consulting. This is something that is going to be recommended after you've done perhaps a little bit of bug bounty or some freelancing, because consulting is where you're actually going out and talking to different businesses and you're reaching out and getting your own clients. And so that's going to be a little bit more advanced. However, you're going to learn how to go about that the right way and how you can get your own clients if that's a route that you want to take.

And then finally, in chapter 14, Anthony is going to give you his real world experience as far as how to navigate the cybersecurity marketplace to get the right kind of job. You know, starting now, or maybe if you have some experience. Right, you're going to have a roadmap for that and then some book recommendations and then some of the best places to practice hacking for free. So this is the entire Book overview here at any given time. This, Of course, may be updated and there may be some additional chapters or chapters added. However, as it stands at this moment here, this is how this Book is currently structured. So I'm excited for you to get started and look forward to seeing you on the inside.

Cybersecurity

Welcome to chapter one and this chapter, we're going to cover what exactly we're going to go over in this chapter, in this chapter, we're going to go over the foundations of understanding what exactly is cybersecurity, what exactly is ethical hacking. I want you to get a foundational big picture understanding of the actual marketplace of the actual type of careers that are available out there and really get you that understanding that is required in order for you to be able to step into a lot more in-depth, more specific topics within the cybersecurity and ethical hacking space. So let's go over exactly what you're going to learn in this chapter. So in chapter one, what you're going to learn is exactly how the cybersecurity market looks at this particular time. And what are the cybersecurity salary potentials when starting out and what is the average cybersecurity salary for somebody with some experience and what you can expect as far as a median salary for the cybersecurity professional.

And then we're going to go over the common methods of hacking. What are some of the most common methods that hackers use and what are the things you should look out for and understand before going into a lot more deeper topics within the cybersecurity field and then the three types of hackers? This is really important here because you need to understand the different types of hackers and which one of these is going to make the most sense for you, because for the most part, you're taking this Book because you want to become an ethical hacker, you want to work for an organization, you want to work maybe as a freelancer or perhaps you want to down the road, do some kind consulting. And so it's important for you to understand what three different types of hackers are and which one is going to make the most sense for you.

And for the most part, it's going to be somebody that is looking to work for some sort of organization or helping businesses out there with their cybersecurity needs. And the next thing that we're going to cover are the four elements of security. This is really important here so that you can understand what these consist of and how you need to navigate these and go about these four different elements of security. And then we're going to cover the differences between ethical hacking and cybersecurity. And you're going to be quite surprised to find out that a lot of times these two get different names associated with them and different definitions. But you'll come to find out and realize there's not much of a difference here. There are little minor differences here and there, but for the most part, there's going to be a lot of similarities.

So then after that, we're going to cover ethical hacking versus penetration testing. What is the difference between these two? What exactly is ethical hacking? How that comes into play with penetration testing as well. And then after that, we're going to go over the job opportunities in cybersecurity. I'm going to show you the type of tires that are involved, how you can get started as an ethical hacker, and then the different job opportunities out there that are available for you in the marketplace. So I'm excited for you to get started here.

Current Cybersecurity Market

In this chapter, we're going to go over the cyber security current market, so we're going to go over essentially some facts and figures here so that you can get a better understanding as to what exactly is going on right now in the marketplace and how you can essentially take advantage and benefit from what is going on currently and the amount of potential that is out there for you as a cybersecurity professional, as an ethical hacker. And so let's go right ahead and jump in here. So one of the first things here is that a hacker attack happens every thirty nine seconds. Just imagine that every thirty nine seconds somebody is getting hacked somewhere. Somebody's out there getting somebody's information, somebody taking advantage of somebody, you know, cell phone, their network security. They're hacking some sort of device, whatever that may be. Right. A hacker attack happens every thirty nine seconds.

So you can see just how much of a need there is for professional ethical hackers. And then since covid-19, FBI has reported over 300 percent increase in reported cyber crime. So this means that cyber crimes have increased significantly. I mean, they've skyrocketed, right, because there's a lot of businesses out there that have shut down their doors or even shut down temporarily. And so all of these different things have played into the factors of their systems being more vulnerable and people, you know, losing jobs, people getting desperate. And so the increase in reported crimes has skyrocketed because of people, you know, wanting to take advantage of the situation as far as the unfortunate pandemic. So especially now the need is going to be increasing substantially for cybersecurity professionals because these are just going to be increasing even more and there's going to be a huge need for the ethical hackers.

And so 43 percent of cyber attacks target small businesses. There's a lot of businesses out there that, you know, have cybersecurity plans. They have strategies. And a lot of times these businesses are the larger ones. Just think about Fortune 500. One hundred. Right. Those businesses that typically have several thousands of employees. Right. They have those budgets to be able to spend quite a bit on their security. And a lot of these smaller businesses just don't have the budgets or are just really unaware of how to get started. And an example of this is I remember a buddy of mine had talked about that his significant other's company, you know, small business had actually been taken over through some kind of ransomware where they were taking over their entire system.

They took over the entire system and they were requiring that in order for them to release the system, the network, that they had to pay some sort of fine, that they had to pay some sort of ransom in the thousands of dollars, I think it was in the tens of thousands. And so this happens quite often because a lot of these smaller businesses are not prepared. They don't think it can happen to them. And lo and behold, it happens to them. And then now they don't really know what to do. And then they go try to find an expert or go to develop a cybersecurity strategy after the fact. So it's important that, you know, a lot of these businesses actually start implementing a strategy and a plan before it's too late. And then 95 percent of breach records come from four different industries. These are the most popular here. So we have the government, we have retail, tech and financial. I mean, this is pretty self-explanatory here.

Obviously, with the government. They're looking to get data. They're looking to get records retail. They're looking to get credit card information, payment information. Same thing with tech, right. They're looking to get, you know, intellectual property. And then with the financial obviously being able to get, you know, records and bank account and credit card information. And then approximately six trillion dollars is expected to be spent globally on cybersecurity by 2020. So just think about that for a moment. Six trillion dollars because of the fact of the increase in reported crimes through the covid-19 and just how much of the cybersecurity industry has grown and is continuing to grow, there is significant opportunity for individuals like yourself that are wanting to come in and get started within this industry. And so here are some additional facts. Unfilled cybersecurity jobs worldwide will reach an estimated four million, about twenty twenty one.

Think about that. There's going to be so many jobs available and they're not going to be filled because there isn't going to be enough actual supply to fill that demand. Right. There's not going to be as many cybersecurity professions. To fill those holes and then you are going to be one of those individuals, if you're looking to obviously take this career seriously and you're obviously here because you want to learn cybersecurity, you want to learn ethical hacking. So you're going to be one of those ones that is able to take advantage of this. And then the average cybersecurity engineering salary is one hundred and twenty thousand a year. I mean, this is a six figure income, right? This is fantastic for obviously yourself or your family for being able to be in the top 10 percent of earners in the country, whatever country you are here in the U.S. and this is definitely putting you in the top 10 percent of earners.

So one hundred twenty K is not too bad. Right. And then more than 77 percent of businesses do not have a cybersecurity plan or strategy. Now, remember how I gave you the story of the ransomware where the company was overtaken by some hackers that wanted to get some ransom because they were looking to get paid and they wanted to only release that network. Right, that infrastructure after they got their ransom. And so this is hyper, critically important here for you to understand that most businesses do not have a plan in place, a strategy. And so it's going to be a huge opportunity to be able to have these if you want to go down into the consulting route, if you want to go into the freelancing route. Right. A lot of these businesses are going to start getting more educated and becoming more aware of the need and the importance of having a cybersecurity plan and strategy. And then the average time to identify a breach in 2009 was two hundred and six days.

This information was gathered through IBM. And so just think about this for a moment, right? You have somebody breaching your network, your information. Right. Whatever information you have as far as your I.T. infrastructure, 200 in six days. Right. Just under a year has passed. Right. Will go by before that individual I.T. the department or the individual company is actually going to find out and know that something has gone wrong. So that's why a lot of these folks don't have the right type of strategy or plan in place or detection. Right. To be able to detect these types of intrusions and be able to stop these before they even begin. And then finally here, only five percent of company folders are properly protected on average. So just think about that. Also, five percent, very, very small percentage of actual company intellectual property, very important information. Right, of that individual company is actually properly protected.

So that means that 95 percent of companies folders are actually open and are vulnerable to attacks. Right. And this is just as simple as being able to do the ransomware where, you know, a hacker can come in and take over, you know, a company's folder, very important documents. Right. Records, and be able to hold that information ransom for them to get paid in order to release it. Right. So these are the cybersecurity marketplace, worldwide facts. I want you to get an understanding of the potential kind of what these numbers are so that you can be prepared in your cybersecurity ethical hacking career. So that's going to be here for this one. And we'll see you on the next one.

The 3 Types of Hackers

In this chapter, we're going to go over the three types of hackers. I want you to get an understanding of what you guys are actually the good guys, which guys are the bad guys and which guys are, you know, in between which are essentially on the borderline. They aren't necessarily good, but they're not necessarily bad so that you can understand which side is what and what these different types of hackers actually spend their time doing and which one obviously is going to be the best for you as an ethical hacker, cybersecurity professional. So let's go right ahead and jump in here. So the first type of hacker that you want to understand is the white hat. Now, these are going to be all of the good guys, right? These are the guys that are actually using their professional experience. Right, to actually help companies, help organizations actually deter hackers from stealing information. And so what these guys are doing is they're using their skills for defensive purposes. Right.

Helping businesses, helping organizations in these white hats are usually professional security individuals that have the knowledge, the experience, the expertise as a hacker and use their knowledge to locate weaknesses and implement countermeasures. Right. To prevent any type of vulnerable attacks. They're the ones that actually ask permission. Right. Get the permission from the actual owner of the data before they're going into and actually hacking the system looking for information. Because what they're really doing in a sense here is a white header and what you're going to be doing as well. You're going to be putting your mind into the mind of a hacker, of a bad guy, in a sense. Right, because you want to think from that criminal perspective so that you can get an idea as far as what type of strategies, actions, plans will the type of individuals that are looking to take over information in a malicious manner.

How are they thinking? What are they perceiving? How are they viewing, you know, this type of system, the one that you're looking to protect, to defend whatever that may be? Right. And then we have the black hats. Now, these are the well known bad guys, right? These are the malicious attackers, the ones that actually attack organizations, companies, individuals that, you know, do the ransomware where they're taking over our company's network companies information and they won't release it until they get some sort of reward, some sort of payment. They have essentially stepped on over to the dark side. Right. You want to think about like a Star Wars type of analogy where, you know, you have the good guys and bad guys. Right. And the black hats are unfortunately the individuals that have turned over to the dark side because there are individuals that, you know, are on the white hat. And for whatever reason, they choose to go to the dark side, so to speak.

Right. And they turn into doing malicious attacks. Right. But as white hats, we're looking to defend, you know, the systems and networks from these black hats. These are the guys that are looking to take advantage of their skill to use it for illegal purposes. They break into systems without getting permission. Right. Without any kind of access. They're looking at how they can gather information, how they can gain access to data and use it to their benefit so that they can essentially get paid in a selfish manner for the release of that information or for whatever, you know, malicious intent that may be. Now, the gray hat, these are the guys that work, you know, on either side of the fence here. They are on the offensive and they're on the defensive. And it all depends on the situation. Some of these folks will often cross over. They are oftentimes self-taught and they're interested in hacking different technologies, different tools, just oftentimes for, you know, out of curiosity.

And so a lot of these folks, they didn't really go to school or get any type of formal education initially. They have essentially, for the most part, and not in every case, have taught themselves the skills of how to hack systems, how to hack networks that have a very diverse set of tools as well as skill sets. But they're more on the curious side and they may from time to time cross the line, over to the dark side. But they're more on the curious side versus the actual black hat, where their actual intent is more on the malicious side. So that's going to be here for the three types of hackers. And we'll see you on the next one.

The 4 Elements of Security

In this chapter, we're going to go over the four elements of security. So these are essentially the four things that you need to understand as far as what security is really centered around and at a foundational level, what really security is about. Because in order for you to be a successful cybersecurity professional and ethical hacker, you need to understand these four components here and these four elements. And so we're going to go ahead and walk through these one by one. So let's go right ahead and jump in here. So the first thing that you need to understand is that all attacks are an attempt to breach a computer system's security, and that security consists of these four basic elements. Now, here's the thing. A hacker's goal is always to exploit any type of vulnerabilities in a system or network to find a specific weakness in one of these four elements of security.

That's why it's important to understand what these four are and the different types of attacks that are generally within these four elements. So let's go right ahead and go into the first one here. So the first one is confidentiality. The second one's authenticity. And we're going to walk into these and some details here and some examples. And then we have integrity and then we have availability. So, for example, a denial of service, right deoxy attack. A hacker is attacking the availability elements of a system and network. For one, they can take many forms. But the main purpose here is to use up the system resources or the bandwidth. So what typically do is they'll flood a bunch of incoming messages, a bunch of overloaded data information to target the system. And so what essentially will do is force itself to shut down, therefore denying any type of service to the actual legitimate users of the system.

So they're going to be overloaded so that owners of the information are not able to access it. That's the availability factor. And then stealing passwords or any other type of data is a confidentiality attack because it allows someone other than the actual recipient to gain access right there, hacking some type of network. And they're looking to get information, passwords, records, whatever that may be. That's on the confidentiality aspect. Right. An element so very important to understand the different types of attacks within these four elements. The next one here we have flipping, for example, these types of attacks are considered integrity attacks because the data may have been tampered with in transit or within the original system. So let's say somebody is using some sort of digital signature software and they send some important document right. To another recipient, you know, a digital signature to be made there.

An attacker can come in and they can actually modify the actual document and they can change up the numbers. And so let's say that it's an invoice or some sort of promissory note. They can go in there and change, you know, hey, ten dollars is what you owe us. Ten thousand dollars is what you actually owe us. That's how the information can be manipulated. It's an integrity type of element that is the factor there. And then finally, here we have the Mac address spoofing, which is an authentication attack because it allows an unauthorized device to connect to a network such as one that is wireless. Right.

Because the Mac address is like an IP address, but it's for your local network and essentially authenticates and gets access to your network, your router, whatever that may be. Right. Do whatever they want with that information. So these are the four basic elements of security. It's important for you to understand what these are and how they can be taken advantage of through different malicious attacks so that you can know what to look for. So that's going to be here for this one. And we'll see you on the next one.

Ethical Hacker Terminology

In this chapter, we're going to go over some ethical hacker terminologies so that when we're going over more information throughout the Book that ties around these key terms, you're not necessarily left behind. No one understands what these mean and what these are essentially used for. So let's go ahead and jump in here. So the first term that I want you to become aware of here is a nice and simple one here. A threat, a threat is simply a situation that could lead to a potential breach of security. Right. Nice and simple, straightforward explanation there and exploit. This is a piece of software or technology that takes advantage of a bug glitch or vulnerability leading to unauthorized access of a system. Right. This is essentially where a hacker is getting access to a system through some type of mechanism. Right. Some type of technology, software, whatever that may be, to be able to gain unauthorized access vulnerability. This is the existence, right, of some type of floor design, execution, implementation within a network, software, whatever that may be. Right.

That is actually leaving itself open to hackers that are wanting to and looking to take over the information, gain access, whatever that may be. Right. And then the target of evaluation. TOEIC is a system, a program or network that is subject to a security analysis or attack. So this is essentially thinking about it from the perspective of a military individual or the military right. Target of evaluation. Just think about a target, right? When somebody says, hey, I've seen the target, the target's over here, it's really just something that is telling you that this is the actual target that we're looking at taking over, going after whatever that may be. And then we have a remote. This is the exploit that is sent over a network and exploits security vulnerabilities without any prior access to the vulnerable system. So this is where a hacker is working essentially remotely, where they are not connected to any type of network and they're just working from really anywhere in the world.

And they don't have any prior access, but they're gaining access to a system to exploit the vulnerabilities. And then we have local exploits that are delivered directly to the computer system or network, which requires prior access to the vulnerable system to increase privileges. Now, like I mentioned and gave you the example of the target of evaluation, a lot of these terms come from the military background, right? A lot of these terms are used in the military because they're very precise terms that are utilized in the physical security realm as well. And so they're essentially tying this over to the cyber security space so that security as a whole can have the same type of terms used for both the cyber security and as well as the physical security. And then we have here an attack, right, pretty straightforward and simple here, an attack occurs when a system is compromised based on its vulnerability. And so that's going to be here for the ethical hacker terminology, very straightforward. Just giving you an overview of what exactly the main key terms are for you to know as an ethical hacker, cybersecurity professional. That's going to be it for this one. And we'll see you on the next one.

Common Methods of Hacking

In this chapter, we're going to go over the common methods of hacking, so what are some of the most common methods that hackers are going to be using to take over information to gain access to networks? What are the different techniques that they use and essentially how they work so that you can become aware as to what you're going to be going up against, essentially. So let's go right ahead and jump in here. Some of the common methods of hacking here we have as a virus or Trojan, and this is essentially a virus within something that you download or install. I don't know if you've ever gone to any type of website that you perhaps had some kind of add on there or had, let's say, like on Yahoo! Dot com, they have a lot of those different ads within the actual news chapter and you click on them and a lot of them say, like, hey, you've won ten thousand dollars or you've won a prize or whatever.

That may be. A lot of times if you click on those, they're actually unfortunately have some sort of malware or virus on there. And when you click it, you run the risk of actually clicking on it. And then it takes you to another screen and it says, hey, your system has been infected. You need to download this software, you need to buy X, Y, Z software, or else your system will be compromised, whatever. It's essentially where you have a virus type of company out there that is telling you that you have been compromised and you need to pay this money to download the software to actually take off the virus. But in reality, all they're trying to do is take your money and then phishing here. This is where websites are replicated to enter login information and password. Right. This is where information is actually gained to be able to take away access to different websites, different login areas. And then the next one here is eavesdropping.

This is where a lot of times, you know, a lot of people think about the government and, you know, what they're supposedly doing, I don't know. Right. I don't have the actual information precisely. But a lot of people say or think that they are being watched by Big Brother or whatever. That may be wrong. But there's a lot of hackers out there that are actually, you know, have the ability to monitor you without you knowing through chapter, audio, whatever that may be, through your specific device. And then fake WAPT, this is where you have fake wifi and essentially get you to sign up to a network and get access to your data because it looks like you're signing on to a network. But in reality, it's a fake network, they're fake wi-fi. And once you sign up, they're getting access to your data and then we have water hole attacks. And so this is more on location specific. And then we have the denial of service. This is where we're flooding traffic to crash a specific site.

Let's say that you have a WordPress website and for most WordPress websites, they have like the actual website dotcom, and then they have for good WP and then Dash or Hyphen Admon. Right, WPE hyphen admin. And any time you go to the euro for that particular website that's hosted with WordPress, you're going to get to a login portal, right? Login page. And so what people can do is flood a bunch of traffic to crash your site so that you cannot get access to your website and actually log in. And then we have the key logger here. This is malware that tracks your keypad. What they can do with this is essentially install it and be able to track what you're pressing on your actual phone or your computer, your device. And let's say if you're logging into a website, they can track what actual keypad numbers you're using, which, you know, are letters. And so they can use that to gain privately secured information and then social engineering.

And this is the psychological manipulation of people into performing various acts or divulging confidential information. Now, a good example of this is just thinking about when or if you've received a text message from somebody saying, hey, free ticket to a vacation or whatever, that may be. Right. You get a random text out of nowhere saying you've won a prize, you've won something. And then in return, they ask you, hey, all you need to do is give us your name, email and birthdate or whatever. Right. And then those individual hackers now have access to your information and they can use that to gain access to your phone, to your devices. Right. And so this is used a lot of times where people are just like they're not. Thinking that people who are out there that are malicious and have malicious intent, unfortunately, that's where a lot of people get taken advantage of because they don't really think the worst or they think that it's just somebody, you know, reaching out to them that is actually letting them know that they've won something. Right.

So this is a big factor here. This is how a lot of people get taken advantage of. And one of the biggest problems we have with malicious intent and hackers with this here, is social engineering taking advantage of people's natural inclination to be curious. And another simple example of this is if you're getting phone calls from like a government or a business, them acting like they're actually the government or a business when they're really not trying to get access to your information and then bait and switch, this is where you have fake ads that take you to a page with the virus, just like I was mentioning earlier as well, where, you know, you have some sort of Web page that you visit and it has an ad on there and it says you've won a trip to whatever or you've won a gift card for a thousand dollars or whatever, and then you click on it and boom, you go to a page that has some sort of virus on there, unfortunately.

And then you have cookie theft here. This is where hackers will take cookies off your computer to act like it's you. Now, one of the biggest examples of this is where a lot of people, a lot of hackers, I would say that use this will typically do it in a malicious manner where they are taking over people's cookies because they're trying to get commission sales from a specific vendor. So, for example, with Amazon, Amazon has cookies. If you sign up for them as an affiliate, let's say you have some sort of blog out there or somebody has a blog or a website where they promote Amazon products. Right. And so somebody lands on the website there. They click on the Amazon product, they go to Amazon.com. They then get a cookie on their computer. Right.

With Amazon's cookie there for, I think, 30 days. And so what people will do as far as these hackers are is they'll steal those cookies and they'll move them over to their own Amazon affiliate account. And so now the original individual, that customer to Amazon, is no longer getting their commission because their cookies have been stolen by these hackers. And so now the hackers are getting the commissions instead of the actual initial Web page or website blog that actually brought the customer to Amazon. And so these are the most common methods of hacking that's going to be here for this one. And we'll see you on the next one.

Cybersecurity & Ethical Hacking Overview

So let's jump into this and go over quickly, what exactly is cybersecurity and ethical hacking? You know, so cybersecurity just put simply, is the act of taking certain measures to ensure that a network and its information is safe. So just protecting your network, protecting your assets, protecting your data, that new computers, that's all really cybersecurity is at a very broad and high level. Some examples of implementing cybersecurity that you might have heard of would be using a firewall requiring strong passwords to log into the computers. Installing antivirus software is also another example of implementing cyber security. So we're talking about ethical hacking. Ethical hacking is the act of attempting to break into a network to uncover vulnerabilities that may be present. So when we say break into not in an illegal way, ethical hacking is a very professional and approved way. You don't do anything without permission.

And we're trying to break into a quote unquote so we can figure out where the holes in the cybersecurity are so that we can fix them. That's the whole goal of ethical hacking. So even though it's technically hacking, you know, it's legal because all the testing is done according to previously agreed upon rules. And those are called rules of engagement. You can go ahead and look this up on your own if you're interested in it. But that's very important when it comes to ethical hacking, because you want to make sure that all the liabilities, you know, are laid out, make sure that you know what you're doing. Make sure that your client is exactly what you're doing and what you're not allowed to do.

What IP addresses, what computers you can touch, different things like that. So if we had to, you know, talk about the difference, then, you know, what would it be? So cybersecurity as a whole just focuses on protecting the network from potential attacks and dangers. Like I said before, this includes offensive actions like ethical hacking and defensive action, which people like to call blue teaming as well. Ethical hacking falls under the umbrella of cybersecurity and is also an integral part of any cybersecurity program. Ethical hacking is a part of cybersecurity. It just tests the network's defenses against tax. And hackers would be launching, you know, so that we can, you know, fix those vulnerabilities that are there before the hackers get to it.

Ethical Hacking vs Penetration Testing

Another topic that is very important to understand is, you know, ethical hacking versus penetration testing, so essentially it's important to know that ethical hacking and penetration testing are actually the same thing. They typically refer to the same exact thing and can be used interchangeably. Ethical hackers conduct penetration tests for their clients or employers. All right. So throughout the Book, you're probably going to hear me use both. I like to lean towards saying we're conducting penetration tests versus saying, you know, while ethical hacking because it just sounds a little bit better. It's a little bit more direct, you know, on, you know, what we're doing. And that's what you'll be doing if you ever become an ethical hacker. OK, so let's talk about some types of ethical hacking, right? There's three different types. The first one is white box hacking.

This is before this is when you do ethical hacking and you have full knowledge of the systems, applications or networks that you'll be attempting to penetrate. So, for example, you know, exact IP addresses, you'll know specifics about the application or the network. You know, you know where you need to look, where some vulnerabilities might be just so that you can test them. That's white box. So full disclosure is what white box hacking is. Now that we have a gray box, we you know, people say, you know, there's like a gray area. This is a gray box. So it's you kind of know some stuff and then you kind of don't. So they're going to give you some information about the network or a system or an application, but you're not giving full details. So this is usually the case when a company like a client might not want you to have full access or full knowledge of maybe their application or their network. So they're not going to give you too much information and you kind of just know how to go about it yourself. So now the last one will be black box hacking, which is proof we have no information at all.

And they just give you, like, you know, a public IP address or they just drop you on a network or just in an application and say, hey, hack this and we know what you can find. And this is the one where you really get to flex your hacker muscle a lot because, you know, you really have to go through the different processes that we're going to go over to make sure that you cover all of your bases, gather all the possible information and, you know, activate any potential exposures that you might find. So now let's go over the different types of penetration testing that you may be conducting if you were to become a penetration testing professional. So there's various types of penetration testing that you might run into when you become a professional. And these include internal penetration testing, external penetration testing and web application penetration testing.

So during this Book, you're going to learn various techniques in attacks and you can use for each one of these types of testing. So first is broadband penetration testing. So this started penetration testing done to simulate what an attacker that has made their way into your network and get access to. Now, it's also a way that companies like to figure out, you know, what's just vulnerable in their network. You know, how you typically would be on site and connected to the network physically or through Wi-Fi or you'll be remotely connected, you know, like a VPN and, you know, given the right to break into as many machines as possible and find valuable, sensitive information like, you know, company financial information, employee personal information, different stuff like that. That's the goal. Kind of like Internet penetration says you want to see what can happen if someone is inside your network to see where you know you need to improve your security.

So now, next up, we're going to talk about the extent of penetration testing. Now, this is inside. Penetration testing is typically done from the outside of the network, and it has the ability for hackers to break in from the outside. So you typically connect this kind of test with a public IP address for the network and try to break in. So you're going to be given a public IP address and we all have a public IP address and Internet. No matter where you are, if you connect to the Internet, you have a public IP address. So technically, anyone on the Internet can find you if you have some type of service running that might be vulnerable and you can see that from the outside, hackers can potentially take advantage of that. So that's why external penetration testing is very important, because, you know, hackers usually come in from the outside and we have something sitting out there on a wall that can literally within an instant launch an exploit and get into your network and then you're screwed at that point.

So now let's talk about a Web application or Web site penetration testing. So this type of penetration testing focuses on attempting to exploit vulnerabilities. In a Web application or Web site and see where is vulnerable, so you want to test this from the outside and from the inside, typically you want to see someone break into the application from the outside and bypass authentication or in someone with, like, basic rights that logged into the application access, something that they shouldn't be able to be, you know, trying to exploit the application. That's something that's very important. And companies care a lot about this because, you know, they might be collecting private information and storing it. They want to make sure that their application is safe because breaches like this, if your application would have a breach, cost companies thousands or even millions of dollars, depending on what, you know, what happened, how big the breach was, different things. So that's why a web application for penetration testing is very important.

Job Opportunities in Cybersecurity

So exactly who is this quest for, you know, what are the prerequisite Books for anyone that has an interest in cybersecurity, ethical hacking? Does it matter who you are? Of course. You know, basic I.T. knowledge is preferred, but if you don't have too much, you should be fine, because when you start, you know, from a very basic level and try to move up. So you're not going to need any prior experience. Truthfully, if you go through this Book and fully understand and learn, you know, what's going on. Like I said before, you know, breaking it down in a certain way in which is going to build as you go through the Book. And you just got to understand and you're going to get it. You're going to be a hacker at the end of this Book.

OK, so what's next? So in the next chapter of the Book, we're going to be going over some networking basics that you can understand, you know exactly how computers communicate with each other on a network, including the Internet. So this is very important if you're studying to become an ethical hack and you really need to understand how computers communicate with each other. So you definitely don't want to miss the next chapter. So appreciate you guys for making it through this chapter. And I'll see you guys in the next chapter.

Networking chapter Overview

Welcome to chapter two in this chapter, we're going to go over the basics of networking, we're going to really get you a foundational understanding of what exactly is a network, how the network works, as far as how a network communicates, how they communicate with different types of information and everything that you need to know about how a network works. Right. So let's go right ahead and jump into the network basics chapter two. So just like I mentioned in this chapter, we're going to go over some of the networking basics so that you can get a basic understanding, right. Foundational understanding of how a network works. So what we're going to be going over in this chapter is what exactly networks are, how they function, what are the different components, the aspects of a network, and then how data travels across the Internet.

It's important for you to know how data travels and what type of forms, what type of form factors so that you'll be able to capture that information as a hacker. Right. As an ethical hacker and be able to put your mind into the mind of a criminal right into a black hat mind so that you can be an effective cybersecurity ethical hacker professional. And then you're also going to learn some important ports and protocols, the differences between a public and a private IP address and really what an IP address is as well. And what exactly are subnets and then a practical example of a typical home network. So let's go right ahead and jump in here into what exactly networks are. So a network occurs when two or more computers are linked together and can share resources with each other. And so on a network, your computer can technically talk to all the other computers on a network.

Right. And so if they're all connected, then they can communicate back and forth and get access to each other to different types of information. And so the good example of a network is the Internet, right? The Internet is the largest network in the world, and it consists of billions and billions of devices that communicate with each other due to their connection through the Internet. So let's go over some of the different types of networks. So we have a personal area network, a pan. This is essentially a convenient one person network. This is typically going to be through some sort of device such as a headset, wireless keyboard, wireless mice, printers. Right. Barcode scanners, gaming consoles. This is where you're going to have a simple, small, very short personal area network. Then we have a local area network, a LAN. If you work in some sort of office setting, then you most likely have been exposed to are aware of a local area network.

This is the most common for a lot of local businesses. And with this there's typically a few different computers that are linked to one or two printers. Also a scanner, maybe a single shared connection to the Internet. I remember years back when I had my office job, I remember the company had four to five different printers in the actual office. And depending where you were working, you had access to a certain printer. So if you were like, let's say, in the north side of the building or the office, then you would have access to one type of printer and scanner. And then if you were on the west side or on the south side of the office building, then you would have access to a different printer. So that's how you can think of a local area network. And then we have a metropolitan area network. And this is essentially where it covers an entire town or city.

And then we have a wide area network A. When this covers typically a geographical area, you can think of the Internet as a wind that covers the entire world. And then the biggest difference between the Internet and many other Panj lands and wins, is that it is open to the public. Right. Anybody with an Internet connection can actually log on and look at specific websites. Right. They are hosted on the Internet. So one of the things that you need to keep in mind here in differentiating the different networks is whether or not they're open to the public. Right. So you want to think about are they public or are they private? And one of the other types of networks that you may or may not be familiar with is the Internet. Now, when I was working in an office setting, we had an online database, which was an Internet for the company itself. 500 employees in the company when I was working in that zone.

And what we had is a database essentially where we only could get access from within the company or if we had access to the company network. Right. And so nobody else outside of the company or anybody else outside of the actual company had access to the actual network or the Internet because it was only for employees. And so that's a private internal Web platform. That holds information data, right, for the actual company, and that can also be susceptible to attacks and where, you know, hackers are trying to gather that information because it's private to that company and then we have a virtual private network. This essentially allows you to change your, quote unquote, identity online where you can have a different IP address, different location, so that you can securely look at a get access to a network, a private one or a public one without leaving any tracks or any traces of who's actually behind the computer.

And so now let's go over the permissions and network security. So here's the thing. When it comes to machines being on a network, right, they're all connected. However, just because they're all connected, it doesn't automatically mean that each machine, each device is going to have access to the other one. And so the only way that you're going to be able to get access to the other information on the other computer or device is if it's given access. Right. If you're given access to that information. Just think about the Internet, you can gain access to billions and billions of Web pages. However, you can get access to every single file. Right, every single page on every single computer that's hooked up to the Internet because some pages are private, some pages are going to be only for internal use. And so just because a device is connected to an actual network, yes, they're all essentially connected.

But that doesn't mean they're all going to be able to have access to each other's information. Permissions and security are central to the idea of networking. You can only access information, like I mentioned, to information and resources only if that individual gives you permission to do so. Right. And so with hacking, which you're essentially doing, you're gaining unauthorized access to a computer network by cracking passwords, defeating any type of security checks, bypassing antivirus, whatever the attack may be. Right. You are hacking because you're getting unauthorized access. Right. And to make a network more secure. Oftentimes, companies, organizations. Right. They will install firewalls. And this can either be like a physical device or a piece of software that's running on your machine, or it can be both.

I remember when I worked for Zones a while back, we used to sell different types of physical devices that acted as firewalls that secured networks. And a lot of times these helped with incoming spam from email incoming attacks. And so if you look at the image on the right, these are essentially walls that are put up where individual hackers, let's say, you know, being able to bypass one stage, maybe they get, you know, some sort of access to information of some sort. They are essentially reaching the actual end of their destination. However, they are getting blocked because there's a firewall right before they have the information that they're looking for. So firewalls are extremely powerful for being able to block any type of attacks, you know, that are looking to gather information, steal data, whatever that may be. As far as having your antivirus there initially or having any other protection, having a firewall adds that extra layer of protection as well.

OK, so we talked about the different types of networks. We talked about the actual network security, the different things that are involved with the permissions, you know, firewalls. And so now we want to go into a little bit more depth as to what exactly a network consists of. And so, as you can see on the right hand side there, that's a visual representation of a network. So essentially here to make a network, you need nodes and connections. And these are essentially the links between then and now. In most office settings, you're going to have wired connections because these are typically going to be the strongest as far as connection speed, and they're oftentimes more secure as well. And so each node on a network needs a special circuit known as a network card. Now, a node is really just a device, right? A network card here is a network interface card that is essentially there to get the actual connection established.

And this is a lot of times through either wireless or wired, it can be both. And so each network card has its own separate numeric identifier. And this is known as a media access control or a land Mac address. And so that code is a bit like a phone number. So any machine on the Internet can communicate with another one by sending a message quoting its Mac code. So this is how these actual network interface cards look like. You can see on the left hand side, there's one for a wired connection. And then on the right hand side, that's for a wireless connection, and especially now there are cards that have both capabilities for wired and wireless as well. And so let's look at the Internet as a network. And so just like highways or railroad lines that connect towns and cities, you know, country, states, whatever that may be. Right.

Computer networks are often very much so elaborate and computer networks are very much the same. They're all connecting networks all around the world. And so the Internet, for example, is based on a set of well defined connections called the Internet backbone, and it includes a vast set of submarine cables under the oceans. And so if you look at the right hand side, the image there at the top, you'll see all of the connections, the cables that are connecting the entire world. Right, so that everybody in the world can gain access to the Internet. Now, as you can also see, there are some areas that don't have as many cables and connections which, you know, lack, you know, some Internet or some sort of Internet connection. Right.

And so when we look at these cables here, it's very interesting to look at that they are just three inches thick and have a total capacity of between 40 gigabits per second and 10 terabytes per second and latencies that are close to the speed of light in just a few milliseconds in duration. So you can see these are very powerful cables here. If you ever thought about how everybody in the world is connected through the Internet, how can everybody, you know, just get online and be able to look at some of these Web sites across the world or get on a Skype call with somebody across the world, is because of these cable connections that are essentially allowing us to all be connected. And so that's going to be here for chapter two, overview of the Networking Overview Network and BASIX. And we'll see you on the next one.

How Data Travels Across The Internet

What are IP addresses? You probably heard before some of you might know, but just to go over very briefly, when you're on the Internet or it's on a network, generally, a computer has to have an IP address, an IP address, just as an ID card kind of identifies who you are when you are on a network. So IP addresses the phone numbers, just how people are going to be able to contact you. If someone wants to call you a city with, they've got to pull it, be a no hit call or type new messages, send it to that number. OK, so it's also important to know that, you know, two computers have the same address, just like you can't have the same phone number, someone else. It's impossible. So now you need to know, you know, how to data. How does data travel across networks? Now, we're going to keep this very high level just to make it very simple and just help you understand data travels in the forms of packets.

OK, so you can think of packets like envelopes. And inside of these envelopes is data that's just packed in there and then they're sent off. Now, each packet, like an envelope, has two addresses attached to it. It has a Swiss address, which is where it's coming from. And then also it has a destination address, which is where that packet is going to go. So now you might know, you know, at your house, you have a router that you're, you know, like Verizon fios or Comcast or someone set you up with a router that connects to the Internet. So this router does what its name says. It routes packets. So the routers read the packets and send them on the correct routes to the destination address.

Understanding Ports and Protocols

So now let's talk about poison protocols, so when data is transmitted over, a network is essentially done over what is called a port, you can think of ports as separate communication channels that hold specific purposes. So each port is going to do a different thing and you're going to use a specific port based on what you're trying to do. So just for example, like if you browse on the web, typically that traffic is set over Port 80 or Port 443 because those are meant for web browsing. And in total, you don't need to know all of them. You only need a handful. But in fact, it's on. If you want to impress anybody, tell them, hey, did you know that there are sixty five thousand five hundred thirty five possible ports? As an ethical hacker? There's some ports that you need to know or at least be aware of because these are going to be ports that you might find during an assessment and be able to take advantage of or just it's going to help you understand, you know, what a specific server computer is doing. All right.

So I'm going to go over some of the top ports and protocols that you need to know. So these are typically going to be called common ports because they're frequently used and they have specific reasons why they are used and are going to be very helpful, like I say, if you don't understand. And so you should probably attempt over to, you know, to commit these ports and protocols to memory or Alisha's however. And also we're seeing it very quickly. It's going to help you in the real world. Don't worry. There's plenty of people at desks who don't feel bad about this because the plain people at their desks have, you know, different kinds of cheat sheets posted on the wall just so that they know because not everybody wants to take time to memorize it. But it will help you to memorize the book. So first up is going to be Port 20 and 21, which is the file transfer protocol.

We're going to keep all of these at a very high level, just as you understand, because all you really need to know. So file transfer protocol FTP is simply what it says is for transferring files. This is a very important understanding of what that point is if you see it open, because it might be something that you can exploit or use when you're doing penetration. So what to do is call a secure show. Now, this is a protocol that superseded the next one, which is twenty three. Tonet So both of these are pretty much methods of remote login. So the problem with telling that was that it was unencrypted. So if someone were to listen in on traffic over twenty three, everything was in plain text. So you can get usernames, passwords, and all kinds of sensitive information. So important to secure a show was created to be used as an encrypted form of remote access to systems.

So if anything is intercepted over twenty two, then you know it can't be read in plain text. It's not something that can be decrypted very easily, easily either. So it's very important to know you should choose point twenty two point twenty three if you unfortunately have three of your computer closets. All right. So next is 25. This is the simple mail transport protocol, also known as SNP. And this is the port that, you know, mail is typically sent over. Next, we have Port 53, which is a domain name server DNS. And this pretty much allows us to map IP addresses. The host names like, for example, Google dot com have a specific IP address, but we might not know that IP address by heart. So we type in Google dot com and then DNS is used to figure out the exact IP address for us and takes us to this site. So this is a high level how, you know, DNS typically works.

Then we have four eighty, which is hypertext transfer protocol, a.k.a. HTTP is just Web traffic and we have one 10, which is going to be the post office protocol three or pop three, as you might have seen him before, is a lot of people calling. This is simply just a port that's used to receive email. So I like to think of it the way I remember it says pop, pop, pop email came in or something like that, like email just pops in or something. That's good. That's how I remember it. You have to remember that way. That's a good way to remember it. The next one is part one, two, three, and that's the network time protocol, a.k.a. NNTP. And this is just the port that's used to synchronize time, synchronize clocks across, you know, devices on a network. So a lot of devices that connect to another device and synchronize the time with that device via this port and this protocol.

So Port one thirty nine is a server message block and pretty much each one of those is SMB. And this is kind of like file transfer, pretty much for windows, but it's also for other systems as well. But you're going to see a lot of it. That's pretty much when you're allowed to map to different drives like you have to map to another computer network and actually go browse the directories from your computer using SMB to do that. For one, sixty one is the simple network military protocol, a.k.a. as an MP, and this is pretty much how a network device is kind of communicating back and forth status messages and such. You don't really need to know. You know, you're not going to be taking in too much of that. But it could be very helpful, as you'll see later on, for justice, for gathering information. OK, part three.

Eighty nine is the lightweight directory Access Protocol, or Alhadeff. And this is pretty much the port that is used with Active Directory for Windows. So it could be useful for penetration. So this is good to know, you know, what that port does because of something that we could use in the future and take advantage of because we definitely could potentially use lightweight directory access protocol to our advantage. Next is Port four for three, and this is just Hypertext Transfer Protocol SIGIR. So this is typically what we're using. We're on the Web. We're using an encrypted session so people can steal our information. We log into our bank accounts online. We're probably doing that over four, four, four, three. And this is securing communications and a port for four or five is another port for the server. Message block is just kind of like in a different format.

We'll understand that a little bit later. Just know that's for four or five and one three nine, both our server message block and then we have Port three three eight nine, which is a remote desktop protocol. And this is how we remotely login to our computers. You can set up for thirty three, eighty nine on your computer and be able to remote into it from another computer on the network over this port. So let's just use it for some kind of remote management and it was left open. The system could be vulnerable to a potential attack. You have to gather the right information to be able to attack it. So now let's go into a little bit about, you know, TCP and UDP. So when using ports, it's important to know that each port exists on both TCP and UDP. So there's a TCP, you know, 80 and UDP, you know, there's TCP UDP for both.

So Tsipi is what is known as a connection oriented protocol, and that's built around, you know, confirming package delivery. So when packages are sent, every delivery is confirmed. And if his and his recent deliveries ever, you know, seem to fail. And so that makes it a little bit slow and EDP, but it's more reliable. Now, UDP is known as a connection with this protocol, meaning that, you know, it doesn't check for failed transmission of packets, you know, as a result is faster, but you might lose some information or packets along the way. So the purpose of this book is just to know that both exist because some specific protocols or some specific ports might be available only on the TCP. You don't need to know, you know, down in the trenches exactly what each one is. Just understand at a high level that they both exist and that you need to be aware of both of them.

Understanding IP Addresses: Public & Private

So now there's going to be public and private IP addresses, so there are two kinds of IP addresses, public and private addresses. So a public address identifies your device, you know, on the Internet, everyone else on the Internet can see a public IP address. And a private IP address is an address that identifies your device when you're on your own personal network or just some private network, something like a home, you know, you can find your public IP address by Googling my IP address, I'd show you, but then you'd have my my my IP address. He might use the tactics from this Book to attack me so I won't show you. And also, you could find your private IP address by opening a command post or a terminal in like Mac and Linux and just type in IP config for Windows or I-F config for Mac and enter and you'll find out your private IP address and all the networks that you're on. So a little bit more so just so that you're aware, you got to memorize this part of the but private IP address falls into typically one of the following three ranges. So I'm not going to say this out, but there are three ranges right here.

And for each one is more like four. As you go down, there's more IP addresses available for each one. And that's just based around, you know, the exact range. So that means like, for example, for the last one, the IP address can be 10 zero zero zero through 10 to five to four to five. That's about 16 million seven hundred thirty seven thousand two hundred sixty IP addresses on that network. So typically, you just need to be aware, you know, so that you know that you're looking at a private IP address. You know, no worries about memorizing these. You can because you will impress people in an interview. But don't worry about memorizing them, like taking an artist, having it written down somewhere, you know, like what a public IP address looks like. Like if you see addresses like two hundred five, four, six, 10, you know, you're going to know that, hey, that's not a private IP address. It's probably a public one or like ten one, ten, nine, ten. You're going to. Hey, that's enough. So just be aware.

What Are Subnets?

So now probably one of the bigger difficulties that people are usually referencing is what are subnets so networks can be broken down further into what are known as subnets. And, you know, as the name implies there, they're just some networks that grouped together specific devices that can communicate with each other. You may have seen it as an IP address, right? Like this right here with like twenty four after it. So actually represents an address range for a 24 subnet. So now let's break this down a little bit, because I'm sure you're probably confused. So here's a breakdown of the subnet and you probably copied this chart down, took a screenshot or wrote it down somewhere just so you have it as a reference. Nobody, almost nobody remembers this typically unless you've been working on this for like 10 years. So let's go over, like, how the IP addresses form and we'll understand something suddenly a little more. So an IP address is made up of four numbers that range from zero to 255. And these are separated by the dots.

You've seen that and the other examples, or you see it right there, too. There's dots in between each of the four numbers. So these numbers are called octets because they are ultimately made up of eight bits. And Bitzer, just one zero sum over that. So all together and address contains you this because we have four octets, which A.K. four numbers, each one of them Ebbets eight times forward, that's thirty bits. Now, when we talk about a 24 network, it simply means that the first twenty four bits or the first three sets for the first three numbers are set in stone. Those numbers are not going to change. This is known as the network address. So we have a subnet like one nine two one six eight one nine zero twenty four. The one nine two one six eight one part is going to be the same for every single address on this subnet, with the only difference being the last octet or the last number, which is the zero that you see right there before this 24.

So as a result, you know, twenty four subnets, you only had two hundred fifty six addresses, a.k.a. you can only have 256 Hossaini. So you can look at the little chart over there on the right and it's going to tell you, you know, the mask, which is what represents, you know, the twenty four. Twenty five, twenty six. That's the network mask that represents that. And it tells you how many subnets there that that specific type of subnet can have and then how many hosts you can have as well. We Arakawa's like I say, you know, just keep the chart handy just so that, you know, you can always represent understanding like twenty eight. Oh what does that mean. And you have this chart, you understand exactly what that means.

The Average Network vs Remote Based

So now let's go to a quick, practical example. So here is a quick Visio diagram that I put together for you guys. So you understand like you know, like what your whole network might look like. So let's say you live in an apartment by yourself. You have a smartphone, you have a desktop, you have a laptop. And that's about it. Maybe you have a smart TV and you want to put that on your. SO as you can see in a legend in the top left, public connections or solid lines and private connections are the dashed line. So remember I told you that when you are at home, you know, you're on a private network. That's the network that you're all the computers in your network typically can talk to each other. They all have private IP addresses. And then what you're going to see here is that your laptop, your desktop computer and your smartphone all reach out to your router, OK? And through your router, you're able to access the Internet. Now, all the devices on your network are typically going to share the same public IP address, when is access to the Internet? This is kind of like a security through obscurity kind of thing that it kind of like unintentional security.

So not each one of your devices has a public IP address that are not technically, you know, all individually reaching out. We're all using specific ports to reach on the Internet. So. All our traffic goes through the router out to the Internet, and then you might go into Gmail, you might go to com, you might go to social media. That's pretty much how it works.

This is the flow, you know, of a typical home network. OK, so now I'm going to show you another practical example. It is going to be a little more complicated. I'm going to walk you through it. But it's a little bit more of a practical example of what you might see for a remote company, for example, like nowadays, a lot of companies are forced to work remote or the companies that already are, you know, thriving. So the next one, the next practical example that I'm going to show you is going to be kind of like a more secure version of, you know, a network when you work remotely is kind of like how my personal corporate network is set up.

Over here on the left, we have, like, you know, users all over the place. Right. Abuses at their homes. They're on their laptops and their laptops reach out to their router and then out to the Internet. So each one of these days is a very different place. We have different public IP addresses. You still see the connection between the user laptop and the router is private to have a private IP address there, wanting to reach out to the Internet. It's public. You see this online. So. You see at the bottom, that kind of represents my setup. I have a hypervisor server called Prox Monks and have a bunch of virtual machines set up on it that I use for work and study purposes. So all of those have a private connection. They're all on my private network at home and they reach out to the router. All those virtual machines can talk to my laptop as well. They reach out to the router and we all share the same public IP address on the Internet. OK, from my network.

So the way that we do it, we have a VPN connection. So we go out through the Internet with our public IP address and then we go into our Adewusi network, which is represented right there by the eight US routers. And then it goes over to our VPN server and this is where we get our private IP addresses, so right here you see all of our user hosts. We all are now on a private network, you know, in the US, and we all can talk to each other. So versus here where we're not on the same network and we can't really talk to each other when we all connect to the VPN and we go through the Internet, we go through the eight US routers and then we go to our VPN. So we all are now on the same network which has this address right here, for example. And then there's other servers on there that you might see in some other places. It might be different kinds of service.

But more specifically, for me, this is like a more security based server, services, and then these reach out to, you know, other tools using our VPN connection. Once one is VPN, we can then connect back on the Internet and get on to, you know, apps like Gmail and such or just browse the Internet. So that's just like a little bit more of a practical kind of advanced, semi advanced example of, you know, a remote base network. So something just to help you flex your networking muscle a little bit, make you think a little bit on how networking works. OK, so now the wrap of networking, you know, you should now have a basic understanding of networking.

And with this basic understanding, you should now be able to, you know, understand how you're hacking them. We want to set up how your own personal network works. OK, so like I said, we're going to be setting up our hacking lab next. So you're going to download and create your hacking virtual machine and you're also going to set up some vulnerable targets for us to exploit. All from your laptop. We just practiced. I am so thankful for reading this far and I'll see you guys in the next chapter.

Hacking Lab chapter Overview

Welcome to chapter three in this chapter, we're going to cover how to set up your hacking lab so you can get started actually practicing your hacking. So some of the things that we're going to cover in this particular chapter is really going to allow you to get the understanding of how exactly we go about hacking into different systems, how exactly the black hats actually work when they're looking to gain access or to do something that is malicious. Right. Some sort of malicious attack. And so what we're always looking to do is step into the mindset of the black individual. How are they thinking? What are they perceiving? How are they going about their plan of attack? And so with us setting up a hacking lab, we're going to be able to step into exactly how a black hat individual would be looking to gain access or provide some type of attack on a network. So let's go right ahead and jump in here.

So in chapter three, just like I mentioned, what we're going to be doing here is learning how to set up our own hacking lab so that we can work through our desktop computer or laptop or whatever device that you have. Most likely you want to have some sort of laptop or some sort of desktop computer. You don't really want to set this up through some type of mobile device or some sort of tablet. You want to make sure that you have an actual computer, right. Either desktop or laptop to work with this type of lab. So the first thing that we're going to be covering here is what exactly are virtual machines and what are the recommended hardware specs to run them on your actual machine? So virtual machines are something that we're going to dive deep into. I want you to really get an understanding of how we're going to use them in our hacking lab and why they are so important and essential when we are actually doing our hacking.

And then we're going to also learn how to download and install Linux into our virtual machine so we can use this for hacking. This is very, very important as well. Kaldi Linux is essentially a must for us when we're setting up our hacking lab so that we can do a lot of the different commands. We can get access to a bunch of different files and do a bunch of other stuff that we're going to walk through in this chapter. And then also you're going to learn how and where to download and install vulnerable virtual machines to hack. So we're going to walk through quite a bit here. And what I really want to get into now is what exactly is a hacking lab? So to give you an overview here at Hacking Lab is a network that you create that lets you practice your skills in a controlled environment. What you're really doing here is you looking to reduce the risk that actually comes from actually hacking real systems.

Right? Real networks. If you look at the image to the right, you see that there's an individual. He's practicing chemistry. He's in his lab working with different formulas and whatnot. That's exactly what we're going to be doing. Right. However, we're going to be using different programs, different scripting languages, CALEIGH, Linux. Right. And then different components and strategies within our hacking lab. So what essentially a virtual lab allows you to do is allows you to practice pretty much any time that you want 24/7. And you don't have to put your data in danger of getting wiped out or getting some sort of virus or malware infection. Right. Because that's one of the biggest things that you want to keep in mind when you're doing your hacking and you're looking to practice. Right. Stepping into the mind of the black , you want to make sure that you're always protected in your information and identities. Always protected. Right.

And so you're also saved from legal troubles that may result from testing on a real website that you don't perhaps do not own. And you may be a little bit curious. You may be stepping into the gray hat area where you're curious about something. I would recommend that you don't get into that type of area where, you know, even though you're not looking to cause any kind of malicious harm, that you just make sure you're staying on the white hat side of things so that you can remain protected and you're not crossing over any lines. And then also, obviously, you get the freedom to be able to experiment and tweak around within your own lab. Right. You don't have to worry about using somebody else's tools, somebody else's VPN or virtual private machines.

Everything is going to be on your computer for you to be able to play with. And so when we're talking about virtual machines, virtual private networks, all these different things that have the virtual right in the very beginning and all these different types of mechanisms and systems that are, quote, unquote virtual, what exactly does this mean? Well, what this all really comes down to is the concept of virtualization. And according to VMware, which I believe is one of the first companies that. Ali started the virtualization industry, and according to them, virtualization is a process of creating a software based or virtual representation of something such as a virtual application server storage and or networks. Right. Look at the right hand side here, this image. So what you have is you have a client, you have, let's say, a computer, and then you have, let's say a program, a virtual desktop like Kelly Linux or maybe some other type of application.

And then you have servers. And so what this is allowing you to do, let's say you have one server and let's say you have 10 gigs. OK, this is just a simple example here. You got one server with 10 gigs. And typically, for the most part, without virtualization, you can only have one operating system on there, let's say Microsoft server or whatever kind of server software, maybe Linux or whatever that may be right on that one server. If you have virtualization, you can actually break down that 10 gig of space and break it down into, let's say, four different groups or three different groups. And let's say if you had three, you can break it down to three point five, three point five and three point five. Right.

As far as space, and then be able to install, let's say, Microsoft Enterprise, Microsoft server on one of the three point fives as far as the operating system and let's say on the other three point five gigs of space, you want to maybe install Linux and then on the other three point five gigs of space, maybe you want to install another software, maybe Microsoft Windows or whatever that may be. Right. I'm just trying to give you an example here. So what you've done with virtualization is instead of only being able to install, let's say, Linux and to that one 10 gig server, you're now able to have three different types of operating systems on that server through the power of virtualization. Right. So virtualization relies on software to simulate hardware functionality and create a virtual computer system. Right. Just like I mentioned, those three point five gigs of space are all broken down to simulate hardware functionality.

And so you have three different operating systems on that one server through that virtualization. And just like I mentioned, this allows the ability to run more than one virtual system and multiple operating systems and applications on a single server. And so this is really something that a lot of organizations, a lot of companies out there use to increase their efficiency, increase their ability to use more of their systems storage and just greater overall functionality. And so for us, we're able to also utilize this to our advantage and have different types of virtual machines, you know, networks and machines on one device when in reality we only have one computer. However, within that computer or that laptop, whatever device you're using, we're able to go undetected and we're able to use several different operating systems and applications within that one.

Machines are very, very powerful. I really wanted you to get an understanding here of what virtualization is and how important of a concept it is for you to understand as an ethical hacker in the next following chapters, Anthony is going to walk you through a little bit more in-depth explanation and overview of what exactly virtual machines are and how we're going to use them to our advantage in our hacking lab and then also how to install Caleigh Linux so you can get started working with your actual hacking lab. So that's going to be here for this one. And we'll see you on the next one.

Understanding Virtual Machines

So what exactly are virtual machines, so virtual machines are exactly what they sound like, machines that are running virtually on your computer now with this technology, you can pretty much run a virtual machine with any operating system, no matter what operating system. You know, your computer is running. The virtual machine is considered a computer that is totally separate from your computer that you're running it on. So we're going to be using this technology to create our hacker machine in our hacking environment. So some of the hardware considerations that you once you consider are going to be pretty much the hardware aspects. So it's convenient, but we have to make sure computers can take it, you know? So I recommend the following specs at a minimum, you know, for your computer to run multiple virtual machines comfortably without too much lag, it's just slowing you down. It's just going to be annoying and hard to hack. So first, you want to make sure that your hard drive has at least 20 percent of your storage available.

And this is because I've seen with my own hard drive that when the space gets really, really low, it doesn't run extremely slow and that's really bad. And you just have to start deleting stuff and then it's just going to fill back up and it's slow again. It's annoying. So preferably, you know, start with the hardest, has maybe like 20 percent plus, you know, storage available. And preferably it'll be a solid state drive. But, you know, the hard disk drives work as well. But I like to see solid state drives. I literally put my laptop on. I used to be so slow that I put

NASA's DNA and it's like a brand new 20/20 computer pretty much. And its computers are like four years old. So I recommend a solid state drive. The hard disk drives work too, you know, if your computer isn't too bad or too old. So you also want to make sure that you have at least a game around. But the more that you have, the better off you're going to be. I personally have 16 gigabytes of RAM in my laptop.

You could do more, you could do the same 12. But eight is probably going to be the minimum because we're going to be doing a lot when we put a lot of strain on our laptops. All right. On my desktop computers. So how exactly do we run virtual machines on our computer? So to run the virtual machines, you're going to need a virtual machine player. And for this Book, we're going to be using something called a virtual box because you can run it on Windows, Mac and even Linux. It's very versatile. So it's pretty much an application that just allows you to load and run images of machines on your computer. And I'm providing you the link right here so you can go really quick in your browser and download it. But I'm going to show you guys what it looks like as well so you can click the link and it's going to bring you up to the virtual box Website.

And depending on what you have, they give you a Mac, you're going to hit the OS X HOHs for Linux. And he's using the fixed pick. Which one is for me? I have a Windows computer and I have it downloaded already right here pinned to my taskbar. But you just click it and then you're going to download it. It's just an X file and then you're going to want to run that and just go through the installation process just like any other software, OK?

Setup Your Kali Linux Machine

So let's meet Kylie Lennox, our hacking machine. All right, Kelly is a costume distribution of Lennix as created and maintained by the Office of Security. It's a company that pretty much is the penetration testing gurus, pretty much of the industry. So it comes preloaded with all the tools necessary, you know, to successfully hack machines. And most of our hacking is going to be done with a Linux virtual machine that we're going to install on a computer. All right. So now let's go through the steps of actually downloading Kylie Linux so you can download the latest cuddliness virtual machine image from the Callisthenics Linux website from the following link right here. You can just visit that link so you guys in a second. So just make sure when you get there, click on the first option of calling Linux 64 bit installer.

So let's go there and check this out. So right here, like I said, the first one, Colonie, 64 bit installer down and then we're going to download it so you can see the ISO files or download and save that. So it's pretty much a downloads folder. Let's get that on here. Well, I have this. I need to download it again, but you're going to download that and then we can get back to setting up our lab. OK, so now let's talk about creating an Uncleanliness Virtual Machine. OK, so to create the colonics virtual machine, you know, you're going to want to open up the virtual box and hit the new button that you see right there in the screenshot. This is going to open up a window that's going to let us, you know, configure the settings for the virtual machine. I'm going to show you in a second. But let's briefly go over to settings that we're going to want to configure. So pretty much you're going to want to enter a name for the machine, whatever you want it to be hidden.

Next, you're going to put four thousand ninety six in. The next box is going to ask you how much, Ramish, you want to give the machine, what, at least four gigabytes of RAM. So it's pretty quick. So you're also going to want to select, create, virtual now create and for the hardest time you could choose VDI unless you plan to use it with another virtualization software like VMware Player or something and keep the storage on a physical disk setting as dynamically allocated to hit next and then give you a machine as much space as you like. Just about 10 to 20 games should be fine and they create it. So now let's actually go through the process of creating this machine. So open a virtual box, we're going to hit new. I'm going to name my machine. Kyly. Very original. I know. And actually right here for the type you don't want to put Linux and your first lead is where it is now. Or you could just put Linux two point six, 64 bit right there.

That's actually probably preferable. And the max, like I said before, four thousand ninety six, that's going to give us a good amount of room. We're going to create a virtual hard disk now because we don't have one yet. Keep it as VDI, which is a virtual box disk image, dynamically ALEC allocated is what we want to choose. And then this is the disk space. You know, I'm going to give it like 20 gigabytes of space. You know, that's not bad. And then create and now we have a calisthenics machine created. So before we got started up, there's some settings that we had to change very quickly. So the structure machine selection machine and then click on the settings button and you know, you're going to want to select storage from the menu on the left and then click where this is empty underneath controller Idy.

And then you're going to want to click this icon and then choose the Calli Linux file that we downloaded earlier. All right. So let's go ahead and do that right now. I can show you very quickly we're going to right click our machine's settings or just hit the button right there is this settings that you click it and then we're going to choose storage on the left. Click right here. Underwear's is empty and the controller clicks the little icon and chooses a disk file and then chooses the father. We downloaded it. So this is my file right here and then I'm just going to hit, OK? And we're good to go. And pretty much what you want to do, you can just hit start and your machine is going to start up. So let's give it a second. Let's see how long it takes to actually start up. There we go. It popped up and now it's asking to select a startup disk.

So we're going to choose the ISO file, although we just chose a start and then it's going to take us a lot of, like, initial setup at some point. So now, before we get into setting up Caleigh, there's really quickly because I notice this. Error, when I did this myself, when I was setting this up, I ran into an error. So if you run into this error on windows where you get this box right here, I'll open up a command prompt as an administrator and just type the following commands. You don't need to know exactly what they're going to do, but it's pretty much setting it up to where much of the box can use the hypervisor potential of your computer. So just do these two and it's going to shut your computer down. And then it started back up and then it should work now. That's what really worked for me. So let me know if it actually works for you guys. I definitely should.

So when it pops up here and it says it has all these options, choose your language. Of course I'm going to choose English. The United States is my location. American English is what I want. So just hit it on all these options that you want. It's just sad. Like I said, a lot of initial settings are very common with Linux distributions. Usually I have to do a lot of this stuff. OK, so now he's asking for the host name. I was going to keep it the same as what I put in the virtual box, just Caleigh and then the domain name. I'm pretty sure if you just keep this blank, if you would like to, but you can name it if you want to. Now, this is asking us to set up the users and passwords and such, so for new users. We're just going to say calisthenics just, you know, keep it anonymous, keep it simple. So the username for my password, for my account is going to be Caleigh and then I'm going to put a password, you know, a super secret password. That's not the password. Don't worry.

The super secret password. Bam and continue. So now it's going to be doing some more setups. OK, so I'm going to choose Eastern for my clock more and more. Of course, I will fast forward through these parts. OK, so right here, just you can put up you can choose any one of these that you want. I would just say use the entire disc just to keep it very simple to enter again. And then right here, just all files and one partition. Not too big of a deal. Finish partitioning it. Right. Change to the disclosures creating your hard drive and then you when you're going to want to go down. Yes. There's nothing on the hard drive anyway so we're using it. So it's not a big deal if it wiped everything off the hard drives, anything on there and where it's not going to break your computer, your laptop.

OK, so when the screen comes up and it says configure the package manager. Yes. Right here to continue without, you know, setting up the network mirror, it'll just give you all kinds of errors. So now it's just going to, you know, install more software, Of course. So by the power of chapter editing, we're going to fast forward. OK, so right here, you just keep this pretty defaults. It's in you. We're just about finished. OK, so now I'm back and it's asking us to install the grubbed loader, so just yes, right here, don't worry about exactly what this is. Click on right here. You see slash dev Celesta.Hey, continue. So once again, we're waiting a little bit more to finalize our installation.

OK, so now installation is complete and we're going to continue with just a couple of important things and then we're good to go. So it's going to reboot and let's get going with our Calli Linux machine. OK, so just make it or it'll automatically do it in like five seconds or something. It's got a load of . Nice, cool dragon, glowing emblem. So now Callisthenics is loading and then it's going to show us a login screen where you're going to put your username and password that you created. So let's give it a couple more seconds. So now I see my username was Califf, in case you didn't remember. And a super secret password. That's not password log in and it's just a computer. So now we have our Lennix hacking machine.

VN Setup & Testing Vulnerable Systems

OK, so now let's go through how to actually set up our virtual networks, sewing machines will be able to talk to each other and our laptops can actually talk to our virtual machines. So what you're going to want to do on a calisthenics machine, in a virtual box window, you're going to want to right click and again click on settings and then click on network and change the attached option, the attached to option to host on the right. So this is going to make a career as a private network with just the host so that, you know, your host has an IP address and your kind of little exposure has an IP address and they can talk to each other. OK. So now let's go through the process of setting up our target machines, so we're going to set up target machines right now. The first machine is called Métis Floatable and the second one is called O.W. Aspey Broken Webapp Machine.

So these are virtual machines that are made vulnerable on purpose, you know, for educational and training purposes, you know, like this class. So we're going to use them as our proving grounds or training grounds in a sense. So you can download them from these two links right here. And you're going to notice that they come in the form of MBK files. And that just means that, you know, we just have to select this file as the hard drive when we create the virtual machine, if you remember that option during the process. So now actually go through the process of doing one of these sounds and click on the link. I'm going to click on Download, it's going to say download. Surely you don't have to click any links or buttons that'll do it for you. So don't worry. So now let's see, let's put this on the desktop, it's safe and it's going to take a little bit of time to download. So once that is downloaded, we're going to come back and we're going to extract it.

OK, so now we have a zip code downloaded. So I have seven zip results. I can be just right. Click here to extract here. And it's going to extract out the Dabic file, as you can see right there into this folder, metastable two Dash Lennix. OK, so that's what a VMDK file is going to be that we're going to want. So once this is done in a couple of seconds, there we go. We're going to open a virtual box. We're going to click on the new I'm going to name it Métis Loadable Spolar. I think so. Change the title to Lennix. I just choose the next two point six kernel version and you can keep these as the defaults because these machines are for performance, so it doesn't matter. So right here is the option. I was talking about using an existing virtual hard disk. OK, so you're going to click the little folder right here. We're going to click and we're going to do a desktop mislabel two and then choose this file right here.

And I see you click on it, Double-Click, on a crate. And now we have a major splitted machine with the right click. It hit start, no start. And it's going to boot up just like, you know, just like the counter machine did. But it's a lot faster because it's already a creative machine. We're just booting it up. OK, and then when you get into the main screen, it'll give you the login information if you want. But really, we just want this machine up and we want to go through and actually do then the host only network settings like we would like for the coffee machine. So let's walk through that really quickly. So for the coffee machine, right click settings, network change from that to host only adapter, right. And we're going to want to do the same thing for metastable. So Settings Network and then host only clicked the wrong one, host only and then we're good to go.

And then you want to do the exact same thing for the Broken Web Apps VM and then we have our target set up and they can all talk to each other. OK, so now this next step is optional. You can do this if you have the capability to do so. But we're going to also want to set up an active directory domain. Whether you do it or not doesn't really matter because I'm still going to showcase the attacks. It is the actuator. I do the main but the main step, the main reason for doing this one as well is just to give you a better idea of what you actually see in the real world if you would have become an ethical hacker or a penetration tester. So we're going to set up a domain controller running Windows seven, twenty, twenty, twelve and a Windows 10 client that's going to join that domain now. And like I said, I'm going to showcase some attacks. So that's why we're going to want to do this.

So I have these links right here that you can go to where you can download the ISO files and just install the virtual machines, just like the other ones that we did. We used an ISO file to install it, kind of like the Sky Linux VM and then you just set it up from scratch. And I'm going to walk you through some of the settings for actually setting up the domain pretty quickly. The project is less than like 30 minutes to do it and then we'll be good to go. OK, so now we're just going to go to the basic setup for Windows Services and 12. So when you get a problem with this screen is to start now, it's going to start the setup process. So you want to choose a second one where you're going to choose the server with a GUI or else you're just going to have a command line except the license terms, custom install. You're going to choose right here and click on next and then it's going to go to the install process is pretty pain free. So just go through this and get back to setting up Barg.

OK, so once that process finishes, there's just going to reboot the virtual machine and you're going to have the Windows logo here and it's going to be loading is going to boot up for the first time. Then it's going to go through some initial setup and then we're going to start to set up a domain controller. OK, so we're setting the password for the administrative account on the domain controller. So a super secure password. That's not the password. The password. Finish and now we have a log in. So you're going to want to send a control or delete, appreciate and, uh, answer Chudleigh right there by putting a super secret password that's going to lock you in for the first time. And it's just like any other computer, when you first log in, still in some setup stuff might be a little bit slow. But what you're going to see is when a server, there's always something called server manager that pops up automatically.

And this is where you're going to do a lot of the initial, you know, setup for your domain controller or just in general, we're going to say, yes, we're here. So we're going to let that load up and then we're going to be able to set up our domain. OK, so from the dashboard, the first thing that we're going to want to do is configure this local server. So one thing I like to do is change the computer name. So going there, click change. I already have it here, but like domain controller, Labbe DC, whatever you want it to be. Unfertilised DC Fellag domain controller. And I'm going to hit OK, and then it'll ask you if you want to restart. So the changes will apply but it'll have to do that right now. We just restart later. It's not really what we do. One of the things I like to do is make sure that I know what the IP address from my devices are. So you can go in here and you can actually give me a static IP address so that you always have this IP address, which is on the network.

So I think our address is 192000 one six eight, five, six, and then we can give it whatever other address that we want. So let's just make it 20, for instance. And I believe that we are going to get all of them automatically or the subnet mask that we want. So remember, this is like a 24 network, so there's only two hundred and fifty six possible addresses for this one. So we're going to hear, OK, on that X this stuff, and then that's some of the initial stuff that we need to do. So now we're going to want to go through and set up. We're going to add up our roles and features to make a choice. We have to make this, you know, a domain control first. So you're going to click on and you're going to click there. And before you begin, just skip this page. If you don't want to see it again, then we're going to do role based or feature based installation. We'll get you this server right here. Don't worry about the IP address.

There's no way about it. That'll change when the computer restarts to the static one that we chose. So now we're going to want to check active directory domain services, Indianness server. So it's OK for us to do our domain services and then also DNS server. OK, and that's all we're going to need for now for what we're going to be doing down here next. And then just hit next on this right here, sheepherding next, and we should be good to go, and then we're just going to restore Mattingley just, you know, to restart if we need to hit a store and it's going to install those features. And now this is going to be our domain controller. So now once this restarts, we're going to go through some more settings to actually, you know, set up the domain and promote it out to other devices on the network so that they can join the network, join the domain that we just never going to be creating. OK, so now we're going to go ahead and get a domain. So we're going to click right here.

And it's a little flag with a little yellow triangle that looks like an arrow click on this server to a domain controller. So now we're going to click on Add a new Forras right here when the option is available. This is going to allow us to name our domain and actually go through the creation process for our domain. So give it a minute and it'll pop up. I just rebooted the computer, so it's a little bit slow. OK, so another option is available. So just click on ADD New Force. I'm going to name this ethical hacking lab that's going to be the name of my domain that I'm about to create. So next and then we're going to want to put a password right here. Don't forget the password just in case you never know. Keep it simple. And that what you're going to click through, everything else is populating all these initial settings for our domain. We're going to hit next.

It's going to check for any prerequisite. It's going to take those prerequisites for any issues or areas that we might run into. So it's verifying that, you know, we're able to make this server the domain controller. So to give this a minute will verify. You can pretty much ignore these errors. I wouldn't worry about it too much. So let's go ahead and install. And this is going to go through the process of creating our domain and making this the domain controller. So let's go ahead and let this lower, then we can determine next steps. OK, so now we're going to have to restart the computer because we did install, you know, active directory service like. And then after we do that, we should be good to go. So one of the things we're going to want to do is that we're going to want to create an actor director or we can create a couple. But really right now, we need to create one for when we do add the Windows 10 machine to the domain. So we're going to go ahead and open up an active directory. So let's see.

We should be able to type it in here and it should come up. Give it a minute. Actors, directors, and computers. So we're going to open that up. Actually, these rams were a little slow. OK, so now an ethical this is ah so you see that we are a domain here and we're going to click on users and then we just right. Click anywhere new user and we give her name. The name is Paw. Victim, you know, you don't really have to give it a name if you don't want to. You might have to actually. So put your full name for the victim and use the login name. That's a poor victim again. And this is probably saying, you know, that's the law line for this domain. And that's their login username. Pretty much so. OK, next, we're going to have a password. Uh, let's see. Just any password, really, obviously keep it a little bit simple. So just, I don't know, password and then password.

And I'm not going to make them change you when they login for the first time and I'm going to make it so that they can't change their password and that it never expires. There we go. Perfect. And they finish. OK, I guess that there are some complexity requirements. So, see, uh, one exclamation point there is I should make it better. I should point. There we go. And now we have a domain account on here for that machine when we do create it. And now then we're going to be good to go. OK, so once you get through the initial Windows 10 set up, you can choose this option right here, domain join instead. And it's going to allow us to join the domain that we just created. So now we need to put in a name. So, you know, we know that this is a victim, Of course, and we're going to make a password for them, uh, just for. And I would just make it a password. One exclamation point, which makes it that one more time, and this is like the local account for the computer and it makes you do all this security stuff.

So go ahead and do that. I'm going to get to it. So when you get this green, you just hit the acceptor, turn off some of this stuff. Like I mean, if you don't want all this stuff on which you probably don't, just go ahead and turn it off, turn all of them off and accept. And then was probably going to load us into our screens soon and then we can do our initial set very quickly with this one, which is going to change the hostname, give it a static IP address and join the domain. OK, so once you have Windows 10 loaded up and you go through, you know, all the basic, you know, initial startup settings for Windows 10, then what we're going to do here is very, very quick. So what we're going to do is we're going to change your IP address.

So what you can do is right. Click on this icon right here, the Internet settings. Ethernet change adapter options. Right click here, properties, and we're going to double click where you see IPV for Internet Protocol Version four and we're going to give it a specific address to use for the IP address.

So nine to one six eight. OK, it's not working. One, two, one , six , eight , five, six, then twenty one. That's what it's going to be for. This one is going to automatically give us a sound mass that we want and we're going to keep the default gateway to where it is. And then we're also going to set the DNS server as the domain controller. This is going to allow us to connect that to the domain so that twenty. Here we go. So now what we can do is we can open up a command prompt. And then we can try to see if we can ping our domain, so let's see what happens. So open a command prompt. So Ping, remember, Meile was called Ethical Hacking Lab and bam, we can pick the domain. So that means that we can join. OK, so now let's actually go through the process of joining the domain now that we know that we can connect to it. So let's go over here and open up our control panel.

We're going to click on a system and security. We're going to click on a system and then we're going to click on change settings right here. And it's going to allow us to change our name on the computer as well so we can change Windows 10 Dash Target and we're going to join the domain. Click the box right here at the Code Hacking Lab.. There we go. That's the name of our domain. Enter this here. OK, right here. That's how big of a deal is that bio's name? And now it's going to pop up with a box that's going to ask us to input administrative credentials. So this is whatever the admin credential you set, you know, on the domain controller. So let's go ahead and try that out now. Super secret password. Now we're now on the domain, so we're good to go, so we hit OK, and now we have a domain where we can. So what we're going to do is we're going to have to worry about that. So we have to restart our computer.

And what we're going to do is we're going to log in to the computer with the poor victim account that we created. OK, so when your computers restarted, you should be a member of the domain. So we're going to pick our other users. I was going to sign into ethics. That's the ethical hacking domain. So what we're going to do. Let's see, poor Victor, and then we're going to put in the password, I should sign it into the domain. And it's going to be an initial log in for the domain, so it might take a little bit of time and it's going to do this right here, even though we were logged in before, because now we're logging in with the domain account. OK, so once all this stuff is done, you're pretty much good to go and you have to remain together and we've got to be able to use it when we start attacking our networks. OK, so now that we have a lab set up and everything is supposedly on the same network, we can go ahead and test connectivity, which is a machine.

So you see some screenshots here. These are showing the command prompt output from when I ran, you know, the IP config. I have config commands. So before we do this, just make sure that they're never going to be sitting because each VM is set to host only mode and then that's going to allow us to test the connectivity by doing a ping. All right. So like I said, you could find the IP address, open up windows and type in IP config or in Mac or in Linux type. And I have coffee and the version of the virtual machines that they're Linux. So I have to find it. OK, so now let's actually go through the process of testing connectivity between these and we actually got that actually works. So I'm going to open up a command prompt that's IPV and we're going to look for one that says Ethan and Ethan adapter virtual box host only network. Some I address from my laptop on that network that is set up is one nine two one six eight five six dot one.

So now let's go over to our political machine. I am config. Now, if your address doesn't start with the same one nine two down one six eight, whatever, as your host, as your laptop does, try to reboot this because you might need to reboot it after you change the network adapter sitting. So just keep that in mind. So now that we know that they're pretty much on the same subnet, I could try to pin one onto the one six eight, five, six, down one. And we're getting responses back. So now these machines can talk to each other. So that's awesome. So just be your reference as well. I want to let you know where you can find other machines that you could practice on. We'll talk about this a little bit and then, Of course, as well. But I just wanted to, you know, offer this hour right now, if you want to expand your hacking lab to test on some things as you learn, here are a couple of options where you can get some virtual machines to test on.

So on Hub Dotcom, they allow you to download virtual machines that were intentionally made vulnerable so that, you know, you could practice hacking. We'll warn you that some of them are extremely hard. So be careful and then also have the box that you use, a site where you can connect directly to a network of vulnerable machines in an attempt to hack into the practice. But the catch is that you have to hack into the Web site to actually gain access to us. That was pretty fun. Don't cheat. All right. OK, so we've got a lab set up. So what's next? So before we dive into the first stage of hacking it is actually essential that we go over some Linux and the scripting basics. So I'm going to quickly go over some Linux fundamentals, Python fundamentals and Basche basics so that you're ready to encounter and use them when you're hacking. So I appreciate you guys for reading this chapter of the Book, and I'll see you in the next chapter.

Linux+Python+Bash+Powershell chapter Overview

Welcome to chapter four in this chapter, we're going to cover Linux bash and Python basics. So this is essentially giving you an overview of the different scripting languages that we're going to use. One of the most common ones that is used in the ethical hacking space is Python, because it's very easy to use, very simple. And we're going to go over all three of these in depth. So let's go right ahead and jump into the chapter four overview. Scripting languages are one of the most important things that you need to also learn within the ethical hacking space, cyber security space, because this is where you're going to be doing your inputs so you can get back information from a particular network, from a particular application, whatever that may be that you're looking to get access to. Having the understanding and experience of these different scripting languages is going to allow you to really be on top of your game.

Because when you can really understand the different scripting languages and the functions and how they work, then you're going to really be able to gather as much information as possible, get into different systems very easily and quickly. So let's go ahead and jump into the chapter for an overview. So what is chapter four? This is where we're going to go over, like I mentioned, some of the few scripting languages that we're going to cover in this particular Book that's going to improve your skills as a hacker. So what we're going to be going over is what is an operating system? I want you to get a fundamental understanding of not only what scripting languages are, but what operating systems are and how they play a major role in how a computer works.

Right. Because we want to take a big picture overview here of how an entire system, how an entire computer laptop works so that you know what you're working with as an actual hacker and where this can make your job a whole lot easier because you understand the big picture here. Right. And then what exactly are scripting languages and the power of scripting languages as a hacker and then some of the basic Linux commands and then the Basche scripting language basics as well, and then also the Python scripting language basics and then finally the power show language basics as well. So what exactly is an operating system? I really want you to get an understanding here, right?

Of what exactly it takes to have a computer device actually run. An operating system is the software that directly manages a system, hardware and resources like CPU, memory and storage. So take a look at the image on the right hand side. And as you can see at the very bottom, you have your hardware. You have your computer. Right. Your computer cannot run without having an operating system because without it, it's just pretty much scrap. Right. You can't run into it and can't function properly without some sort of operating system. And so within an operating system, you're going to be able to have different applications. So, for example, let's say for hardware, you have a Dell Computer or an HP computer. Right. And then you have, let's say, Microsoft Windows. And then for an application software, let's say you're trying to run Skype. So that would be the application that you're able to access through your operating system that is on the computer and then the user.

Right. That would be you. So you have the hardware and then you have the user. Right. And so the hardware is the computer. The actual physical, tangible computer operating system is what allows you to be able to run the computer. And then the application is something that you use within the actual operating system. And then the user obviously is yourself. Right? Just think about an OS, right. Operating system like a car engine. Car engine can run on its own, but it becomes a functional car when it's connected with the transmission, axles and wheels. Right. And so without the engine running properly, the rest of the car won't work. And so the operating system is that engine. It's what allows the actual car. Right. Which in a sense would be the actual physical computer. It allows it to run properly.

Right. And so this is essentially what an operating system is. And so now let's look at what exactly are scripting languages. And so a scripting language is a programming language that is designed for integrating and communicating with other programming languages. And so you look at the right hand side over here, this image, this is how most programming languages will look. You have a lot of inputs. You have a lot of commands that you can use and inputs to get back specific information. And the two main ones that we're going to be using here is the Basche, which is the scripting language within the Linux interface and then the Python. And this is the free open source, actual language that is the most widely used in the ethical hacking industry. And it has a ton of libraries that can.

We use it for both hacking and for writing very useful programs, right? Python is one of those programs that can be used for a ton of different things. However, for purposes of this Book, we're going to be using it to get access to different information, to input different commands. And so that's going to be here for the chapter for overview. You've got an understanding of what exactly an operating system is, how it functions, the importance of it, and then also what exactly are scripting languages and how we're going to use these to pull up different information and get access to different files and data as well. So that's going to be here for this one. And we'll see you on the next one.

Linux Basics

What exactly is legs, so legs is an open source free alternative operating system that can run pretty much any hardware. So if you have, like an old laptop somewhere, you can wipe it clean and put Linux on it entirely for free. Typically, Linux is very lightweight and it's very secure by default. Of course it has vulnerabilities, but it's a little bit more secure than other systems by default. And then also it's typically command line focused. But you can also, you know, get a distribution of Linux that has, you know, Buist. So there are hundreds of different flavors as people call in the industry. These are just different versions of Linux and you can just search for them on the Web and you can find them and see which one, you know, fits you the best, but the one we're going to be using for this horse and that you would most likely be using, you know, if you were doing this. Hacking is called Linux, and it's designed primarily to be used for penetration testing and ethical hacking.

So let's just go over some of the basics and Linux, you know, so the terminal. So a lot of the things that you're going to be doing, Linux, is going to be in line, especially with politics and hacking stuff. So you're going to have to get used to it, you know, get used to staring at the black box. All right. And just the lines and lines of code type stuff now so that you're not really going to be looking at just going to be looking at the different demands and outputs from it is not anything to say. Don't worry, we're going to get into Astarte, very basic. So to access the command line, you're going to need to open a terminal. So what you're going to want to do is click that black box you see up there that has a white outline on it and it's going to open up a terminal from that terminal. We entered commands.

So I have a list of some of the basic Linux commands that I want to go over, which you guys there's a handful of commands that you need to know. You don't have to be like a Linux master to become an ethical hacker. But there are some commands that you really do need to know. And, you know, just note that Linux is case sensitive all the time. So make sure that you're inputting commands exactly how I, you know, show the show, you know. So just to briefly go over some of the commands. So who am I to username the current user hostname press the hostname or device press the current directory that you're in, which is just a folder else list out the contents of the current directory that you're in could be followed by the directory name. It changes to that directory. Dot backs up about one directory. So like if I'm in the homeslice user folder, if I post a CD entry, it'll take me back to the home folder.

OK, so my dear. And then a directory name. So this creates a new directory, R.M. file name at least the file name that you indicate right there. And then there's RDR delete the least integrated directory Asou Dasht username. It'll allow you to switch users like in Windows. We typically have to log in and out in Linux. You do a command line and it's very, very quick. You can just as you dash use the name and then you're good to go. But in the past, what were you good at? And then any command excuse that command with room privileges, which is the same as administrator privileges of a pseudo dashi, allows you to switch immediately to the root user account. And history shows a list of all the reasons commands that you have executed. So I have config prints out the IP address and network interface information for the system. And then S.H., MIT and ABC right there is going to be like it's going to be three numbers by the there of a placeholder and then the filename so that I'll change the permission of the indicative file and we're going to go over that.

So now let's go over to our colleague, the next machine and actually try some of these commands. OK, so we're the home screen of our colonics machine. So this is the terminal box right here. So click on that and then it should open up a terminal window right here. So let's go to the commands that we, you know, just went over and I slide really quickly. So you type in where my inner ear tells me that's my username to see the current username. You know, the answer to that executed that command. So now let's try the hostname command post. They remember I named this box tally. So, Of course, the present working directory. This tells me that I'm currently a home county voter and if I wanted to see what was in here, I'm not sure there's anything in here. There is less and less of the contents of the directory. You can add different switches on anything else I like to play.

It shows all files and lists them out vertically and shows permissions as well. So that's something that I like to do. Something you will probably find useful as well as other Haggard and then so let us see it as a blessing in. So if I want to change to the documents folder, its CD documents, and then switch to documents for voters to affirm that Puedes when

Homeslice counted such documents. So now if I wanted to go back because the SAS should have on record a CD space dat dat and now I'm back in homes like California. There you go. So if I want to make a directory called, you know, hacking tools will do media hacking tools. And now if we do, unless we see that as a directory there with the switch to it's a CD hacking tool. So that's pretty cool. So that's backout. So let's say that we wanted to remove her file, so I'm just going to make a fire really quick. This is another listener. It's called Touch and then a text file. It just makes a file. So the Nici test file is right there.

So what we can do, we can remove this test file. So if one is deleted because it was a mistake, you know, R.M. and then the test file and now the test files are no longer. There you go. So now armed are the other remote functions we can take. We can get rid of the hacking tools that we need. Oh and also at any time with Lennix, this is a quick little nugget. You can hit tab when you start to type things and it'll autocomplete it for you as very useful. We don't need to try to rush or it just makes things a little bit easier and you get into the flow a lot. You'll start seeing that using the tag function a lot. But anyway, so armed you are, hacking tools are no longer there. So now let's say I wanted to switch to another user. I don't think I'm another user here, but let's see if DSU Caleigh and then you put in a password, super secret password and it switches to that user. I don't think I have any other uses here, but we can do a pseudo dashi and this will allow us to switch to root them. And now I'm the root user.

And if any time you switch users or anything or you switch to room, you just type in exit and you can get right out of it. So also, if I wanted to do like let's say like this directory here, I can see right now and list out the directory, everything is in it. But if I didn't have rights to this folder, like maybe it was owned by Rupert and I couldn't see any of this stuff and I couldn't see this coming in here, I would do a pseudo command and then I would do less. And typically the pseudo command will also, depending on how your system is set up, it'll ask you for your password, but it doesn't always do that. But also note that when you do, you start last, I'm not sure the exact time interval, but it lasts for a good while after you do Souto and then you want to do it again for a while until you don't execute any commands for a while. So moving on to the next command, let's say we want to see what we've been doing because there's something I did earlier that I need to do because I need to see it. This is very helpful.

So you type in the history enter and it shows you the history of your commands. So then I have config, which is going to show us our networking information. So the way this country's VM is set up is different from the older ones. You actually have to do pseudo. I have config and then it'll show you everything is set up a little bit more secure than the older ones were. So we have to destroy them disruptively then. You might not have to do that. But the way they set these, you have to. So now let's make another five really quick because we are in the homeground, so let's make another file. So touch the test file too, just because we see the test pilot who is there and we see sorry else. Just so sometimes it gets a little bit overwhelming. We do. l'Est, L.A. so with the test file too. So you can see that the owner of the file, which is Calli, we see equally twice. So the first one represents the owner of the file. The second one represents the group that the file belongs to.

So the owner of the file has read write access, which is represented by the RW that you see there. And the group actually has read access and then everyone else has read access as well. So this is typically how you'll see Linux permissions and that's how you would interpret them. So we can change these permissions, if you want, with the C H Marchman. So besiegement and then those numbers I talked about before where the ABC was the placeholders. So let's say we want to make sure everybody can see and read this file and execute it if it's the executable file, we can use 777 and then test file two and now Tesfai to execute a moulis when it color changes. And now everyone has read, write and execution access access look are more specifics of the Linux permissions. I'm not going to go over them in detail here. Gonna confuse me, but I'll include something in the resources for you guys to be able to go learn a little bit more about Linux permissions, because it's something that's very important to learn as well.

Working With Directories & Moving Files

OK, so now let's just go over some important directors that are really great that you should really be aware of when it comes to lyrics. So when you just see slash, that's just a deregulated system where, you know, everything starts. Every file and folder is included in this directory then is slash XY. And this contains, you know, just system configuration files. Again, it contains executable binary files, you know, all these stalled applications. And then its Ezzedine contains the executable binary files, important system applications. There's this vast, large log folder and it's typically where, you know, different assist logs or logs for the system are stored. And then there's the slash and then slash username, typically the home directory for the specified user. And this is created if you create a new user, it creates this directory for them by the fall and if you go to login and automatically puts you there as well. So now let's talk about copying and moving files.

This is something that's probably pretty important as well for you guys. So there's the CPM in the file about a file name and then a path. So it's going to place a copy of the indicative file and you can use a directory and pointed out file as well if you want to. It's kind of a personal preference, but it's for me. I like to be in the directory, the file I'm trying to copy and then copy to somewhere else. So that's what I would like to do. M.V. file name and then the path where you want to say that it moves the initiative file to that path so it doesn't make copying just moves it. So once you move it, it'll be pretty much deleted or removed under a folder that's currently in. So yes, please, though, don't forget that it's going to delete the file folder that it's in right now. Don't mess that up. So let's go ahead and test this out really quick. OK, so we have our test file here. So let's say we want to copy it. So C.p and then you're going to do test file two and then you're going to choose the path.

Let's say we want to put it into our desktop folder. We went and you saw it actually popped right there in the desktop test pilots who's now there. Now, let's say that was a mistake and we want to move it back. So let's say we want to move and we'll try this from here. You can switch to the same directory, but we can do it from here to you can do it from anywhere, really. So desktop slash test, file two. And then we're going to choose that. We want to put it back home, slash Câline and then it's back in. This folder is no longer on the desktop. So that's some of the basics of, you know, just copying and moving files. Pretty important to know.

Installing & Updating Application Files

OK, so now that we know some basic witness commands, let's go over how we can install and update applications and files. So the Apte Dash install, followed by an application name and looks online through different repositories that you have linked to your system for the application name and then download and install it on your computer. The APD dash gate space update command searches, database for files and applications that can be updated and then a dash gate upgrade option actually upgrades or updates the applications, you know, that were found from the previous command. And then if you ever need to upgrade the distribution, which like, you know, like a new version of Linux or something comes out or maybe you have a move to a new version of Bill to this comes out, you do a dash it dist dash upgrade and I'll allow you to upgrade, you know, the distribution to the next version. So now let's go over and try a few of these commands.

OK, so let's first try to install an application so you can try and make sure that you when you try to install an application, because typically you're going to need route access to, you know, to install an application on a device. So this is a pseudo ABC dash install and this is just a Web server application that you could use, you know, for some hacking stuff in Fiji. So let's do that. So it's already started here. But if you look online and check, hey, it's our newest version. So if I didn't have it installed, it would go through and actually do the installation process automatically. So now let's try a pseudo ABC dash git update. So it's going to look online for live updates. So now let's do a pseudo ABC dash upgrade. And pretty much since it didn't find anything to update, it's not going to be able to.

Linux Text Editors

OK, so now that we know some of the command line stuff, let's talk about some Linux text centers. So Linux has various tech centers that, you know, are typically installed by default and you can use them to enter your files. There's V, which is my preferred text editor, all really old school, a little bit more difficult to use, but it's so very powerful. If you learn the different shortcuts and commands and such then as VM, which is just an updated version of the improved user interface and just some new features. There's Nano, which is user friendly, and you should probably start out with NATO if you're a beginner. And then there's also a leaf pad, is there? Sex ed uses the graphical interface for editing, which is more similar to what you're going to find, you know, like with Windows or something. And you can also just try, you know, if you need to download it a bit, actually install each pad and then you'll be good to go. So you'll choose pretty much which one of these you want to use.

So I recommend that you don't play around with them and see, you know, what works best for you. I'll show you guys really quickly, what each one looks like and then you can choose from there. OK, so we're back on the Linux terminal, so I'm going to show you V and then I just do. I still have the test file here. So this thing, the test file now. So this is a very, very basic kind of almost clear terminal and allows you to type. So what you need to do with V, you have to hit the entire key or the IP typically before you can actually start to type. So when you see insert mode down there, you can actually start typing. So if I type in, you know, hey, this is a really cool class. When are you going to teach another? There you go. So when you're done typing and inserting something into me, you can escape. And then now, no matter if you hit keys or anything, you see them popping up at the bottom.

It's not going to answer them in the file because I'm no longer in certain mode. And with V, you have to be outside of consumers. So you would hit escape. And if you want to save the file, you would do Colen and then you would do it right. And that saves the file. So now it says as written, so save the file. So then when we quit, you can also Lyness these commands. They said if you want to write and then quit afterwards, you can do it like this and then quit. So now let's actually look at a test for this. Another Linux command is very useful, such as Sceats Cat and then the filename and a little like print out on the screen. What's inside of that file? So there you go. Hey, this is a really cool class. When are you going to teach? Another day. You know, they are pretty much the same thing, just with different features. So it's not really worth showing because then there's Nanos a little bit different.

So now it's as far as a little bit more of like an almost Buie type of feel was a little bit easier as some of the commands down there just so that you guys know exactly what to do. And when you see that little carrot, it just means that you have control. So if I want to say the control oh is going to ask you the following name, you could change that if you want to enter. Now, I wrote the file and then you get control X to exit the go and then is also. So as you can see, Leaford isn't installed here, but that's no problem. We could just do a pseudo ABC dash, install the pad. OK, so as you can see, we're not going to be able to install Liefeld on this version of colonics. We'd have to go and update the sources list for the repository that it pulls from in order for, you know, this distribution to find it.

But what we can do is we can actually use a different sect that is already on here by default. So if you just click the little Khaliq on appearance's text editor and then bam, you have a text that is just like you used to like on Windows or OSX and everything. So that's definitely an option on something in the resources. If you guys want to actually learn how to go and edit this file, because it would be good hands on and kind of like an experiment for you guys in a little lab to go edit a file and see if it works and try to update and install the application.

Searching For Files

OK, so now let's go over some of the basics of searching for files, Lennix. Just a few minutes to go over one that you can use the location, followed by the founding man and first, such as the computer, is built in the database that it has called for that indicated file name. And if anything on the file system ever changes, like you asked for new files or something, you can always update the database manually with the update DB Command from the Green Line, then that's fine, followed by a directory and then Dasch name and then a file name. First search is a specific directory for indicated Filoni. So you would use this if you know where you want to look and then what the finding is exactly. Then there's also the Wichman followed by the filename searches through the directories that are defined in a path that in the path and binary variable, which is something Lennix is calling a variable that's like always present and usable in the command lines, kind of part of the Basche language and its search.

Is that for the given filename? OK, so we know that we have our test file too here. So let's do a test file too, so it doesn't know. So let's try to update the command update DB or ASUDA Update DB. He never accessed this. OK, so now let's try to locate again, and now he knows that a test file is. So now let's try to find just the same exact one. So we are in Hoagland's. That's fine. Slash home slash alley and then dash name and then file names of test file two and bam, it found it right there. So now let's try which command. This might not work because I don't have anything and might not have anything stored in there. So which in test file two is not going to find out because I don't have directories in the path of my variable. But if you were to set that up with search, do that and be able to find the file for you.

Bash Scripting Basics

OK, so now that we, you know, got past some of the basic command stuff, let's talk about scripting basics. So actually, actually the language that used to navigate Nesquik commands in Linux. So all of the demands that, you know, we've learned so far actually use the scripting with no modifications in them whatsoever. So congrats, because, you know, better scripting now. So all you need to do is use those commands as a basic knowledge of Basche syntax. And we're going to automate processes in no time like anything that we did. Now, you can literally do that with a through so you can open up your preferred editing application and, you know, get to work on some of the stuff that I'm about to show you right now. So here's the basics. So all backslaps typically start with this Pain in an exclamation point, slash slash bash, and that's at the top of the file. You're going to create an actual best script as a file.

So you're going to want to make sure that this is at the top every time that you make a battlegroup. Dispersion tells the system what it's going to run this file with. But this could be slash being slash python or something. It was Python. But right now, who needs Basche? So that's what it's going to interpret all the following lines of code as. And just remember that the fans are going to execute in the order that you put them in. If you want to declare it variable, you do the variable name equals and then your value. If you want to access it, you would just write a dollar sign followed by the variable name. If you want to print something out, you know, on the screen, you would just write Echo and then the parentheses and put your text in there or you echo and the new variable name. So let's go try some really great Lizzio, but a new file and V Basche practice. OK, so we're going to go on to answer mode. Remember we start close to the Palestine exclamation point, slash bean slash fast and now he knows to interpret this as a bad script.

So we make a variable called this class and then we're going to be equals and we can do single quotes right here or double quotes. I want to say this class is super fun. And I'm going to tell my friends about it. There you go to make sure you do that. So now let's go down and let's actually access these variables. So echo dollar sign and then the variable names of this class. So now I hit escape right quick. Bam, Alice. Now, what are you going to see? Is that the best practice? I actually do not have an execution. Right. So what we can do is a mild shortcut, which would be Siegmund plus X and then the name of the file. Best practice, bam. And now the color changes and we have actual execution access. So the way that we can run this bash is done slash best practice. And hey, it echoed out. This class is super fun and I'm going to tell all my friends about it. So make sure that you guys do that right.

So that's just like some basics in the syntax. So now let's go over functions in bash. So to create a function and bash, it's going to look like this. You had the function name and then two parentheses and then these curly braces and then you put your commands for the function inside of it and all the function. You just type the function name. It'll do the function. So if you want to create a function that takes in an argument from the command line, you just get the function name again and then echo. So here we have Echo. This is the random number today and then it has signed one so that on one sets the argument given that the command line to that variable. Right. So whatever the first argument that you input at the command line after you put dot slash and then the filename and the space and maybe you type in something else, like you type in like a random number, it would actually use that as the variable.

And we can use this one specifically, we could just use the random variable which is in Gibby and Linux by default, and you'll be able to just pass on a random number. So let's actually go and try to make this OK. So I'm just starting to follow the bash function. So remember, we have to start with the policy points that have been bash and then we can go down. So I don't want to set a variable equal to our first argument that we're going to pass in. So numbers that equal time once and now, the name of our function, which would be a pass argument, I say that parentheses and curly braces. So now say echo today's user provided no is and then you can put no. There we go. Right there. So Cityscape quit. Well actually sorry. Before we do that, Of course we have to call the function which makes sense. So let's go ahead and call the function. So pass argument is all you have to do is quit, give execution access.

Sejima plus Xpress function there. Oh so dot slash function and let's say seventy six five for every go. Today's provision provider number is seven six five four. So now you know kind of like the basis of creating a functioning Basche. OK, so now let's go over capturing user input. So the input from user and stored as a variable we would use the Grand Redzepi, whatever text you want to print out, and then a variable name and read input from user solidly from passwords stored is variable. You would say redoes Espie. They need this X you wanted to print out and then followed by the variable name. OK, so now let's go try this out really quickly. OK, so I'm going to start a new file, the C v input. Keep it simple. So let's put our command here first slash bash. So now let's read the SPI username, keep the symbol and per user as the variable when a star dies and read Espie password passWD.

So now we can echo these because of the story's variables now. So let's say now this echo, you know. Thanks. Or say thanks and then username, so say thanks, user, your password is now password. There you see my plus X and put the wrong plus X inputs. Got such input. Not as from your username. So Anthony password. Password. Thanks Anthony. Your password is not their password so now you're not taking user input. And I'm just going to give you guys an example of, you know, a conditional statement in Basche really quickly. So when you see, you know, dash alti that means less than. And then if you see Dash G.T., that means greater than. So this one is asking you. So it takes your input, and asks you how old you are.

So what's your age? And then it says if the variable age is less than 16, then you're going to echo you are young or else if which is like saying like another if statement. If the age is greater than 60, we're going to say, hey, we're going to print out your maturity. Other than that, we're going to go out, you're in the middle and then fee and the additional. OK, so that's like, you know, kind of basic of that. So and that's, you know, Basche kind of in a in a nutshell, you know, it's a lot of conditional statements and just using a different syntax and commands to execute things that you want to do this, it can go a lot deeper than we did and you can go out and learn that on your own. But that's pretty much the basics of Vash.

Python Basics

OK, Senator, we did bash. Let's go over Python basics, so Python is one of the most utilized scripting languages in that community, if not the most utilized. This is due to its simplicity and power because it's pretty much almost like English. It's a little bit easier than the Bashkim thing is. And it's very, very powerful. You can literally do anything that you could imagine with Python. So it's very easy to pick up and it's going to drastically help you with your acting career, any career that you have in cybersecurity generally, because Python is used typically, you know, to automate processes, you know, in gigantic enterprises. And it's very, very valuable to know Python. So we're going to go over the basics. And since, you know, a majority of the experts that you're going to see are written in Python, being able to read it and, you know, know what's going on and how to modify it, it's going to be key. There are some basic Python syntax.

So Python scripts in Lennix start similarly to the bad ones, except this time it is going to say user in Python. That's going to tell the system to interpret this as a python script when it runs. So if you want to declare a variable here, which is variable name equals value, when X is variable, you just type the variable name. If you want to print something out on the screen. So he's an echo. In this case, we would use print and then we would put the parentheses signs and whatever text that we want to put inside of it. OK, so let's talk about creating functions in Python. So if you want to create a function, you start with def and then the function name with the provinces and then colon, and you would then start defining your function. And if you want to call the function in Python, you need a function name followed by two parentheses and of all the functions.

So if you want to create a function that actually takes in an argument, you would just do the naming of function and you will put the argument right there inside of the parentheses you would use that you would access that variable, you know, with the ARG one variable in this case because it was passed in in parentheses. And then as you pass on those parentheses, you would be able to use inside of that function. So, yeah, this just prints out. So this one principle, you know, you passed in and whatever the argument is right there. So all this function from the command line would probably look like function, the function name, and then you have the in parentheses and inside the quality will put my name. And that would be the argument that you passed in. So let's actually go and try this out. OK, so I'm going to do a new file. So the python peepy function. There we go. So let's start with our command.

So is countersign at some point as viewers are so experienced, Python so now knows that this is a Python script. So A.F. and then our function name, let's say it is to you, just name, keep it simple and then our colon and then we're going to start to make our function. So it would just, you know, if we wanted to print something out, so. My name is Anthony. There you go. So that's the function right there. So then I would be able to call the function like this, you know, right away. So now we can do C.H. Mod plus X PI function and now we do dogpile function and say, my name is Anthony there. We created a simple function. OK, so let's say that we wanted to pass something into dysfunction. So we'll go up here and in parentheses, input, maybe name and we would take our name right here where we have it right now and we do plus name and then less. When we call the function we would actually, you know, probably want. So this Anthony. So now, right now, let's try to run it. That's the slash PI function. My name is Anthony.

There we go. So now we passed a function and we passed in something into Python. OK, so if you want to capture user input in Python, you would just set it up like a variable. So the variable name right here is user input. And then that method from Python is input, parentheses and then input is what is going to print out on the screen and wait for you to actually type in your input. And you can print this by printing the variable with the print command. That would be a lowercase period there as well. So now let's actually go over and try to do this, starting new files of the PI input. So we're going to insert our common user in Python. So now that's a user's keyboard like it was in their user input equals input. I say insert your age and make sure we have parentheses around that and let's make sure that we spell input. Right. And then we're going to print. User input. There we go. So I was in a very quick siege mode. Plus x pi and put Bam that slash PI input and see your age.

Ask me how old I am. Let's say I'm 28 because I am. Yeah now I'm 28. So now we know how to cash and put it in, print it out. OK, so just like Bashour and give you an example of a conditional statement in Python as well, similar to the other one. So in Python, this is how you would type this. You would say, you know, if for example, five is greater than 10, you print out, five is greater than 10 in text or else print five is less than

10. So in that case, five is not greater than 10. You're going to print out five is less than ten, which makes sense because five is less than ten. So this is otherwise a little bit simpler when it comes to, you know, making the conditional statement. So you kind of see that python is very simplistic in a way. So now let's talk about for loops.

So this is another iterate through maybe lists of different things. So like for this example, right here, we have a list right here called Fruits. We have apples, bananas and then cherries. So if we want to access all those values inside of that list, we would say for X in the fruit colon and then we're printing X. So X in this case is, you know, each individual, one of those. So for each individual thing inside this list, inside the fruits list, we're going to print it out on the screen. There's another way that you can use for loops as you print out every letter in a string. So right here in this next one, we have four X in and then parentheses my string. So it'll take each one of those characters, including the space, and print it out on the screen. OK, so one thing that you're going to notice, Python is used for a lot. You're going to be noticing that you're like some of the experts that you're looking at, they're going to be connecting to, you know, something called sockets.

And this is just simply creating, you know, connections over specific ports. Think back to our networking chapter, to another computer using Python. It's very important, understand, because, you know, it's going to allow you to quickly connect to ports on the go or be able to understand and explain changes. You know, if you need to like porridge, change something, maybe some syntax is wrong. We'll do it. So here's an example, Python script for, you know, connecting to a port. So you see our recommended top. So then we have an import socket and then we have IP as a variable and then it says more input. So let's say that actually to put the IP address. So it takes it as more input and then you have the port which you took as input into port in. And this is also a user captured input. And then we have another variable that's going to be this is the line at the nexus to the port.

So socket socket. And then these commands right in here are going to allow you to connect to a socket. So the way that we would actually make this connection is using the . So if you connect underscore X and then you put those two variables in there, the IP in the port, then we will present, you know, the port and then say that that port is actually closed. So this is a way to check to see if you can actually get to this port. If you can get to it, then I would say that it was open. But in this case, you know, if you can't get to it, it would say that it's closed. So that's like a basic overview of, you know, how you would actually connect to, like different ports if you wanted to, like, you know, maybe do like a manual port scan, which you will probably never want to do. But if you want to do something like that, you know, you will be able to check to see if a port is open.

If you want to check on a fly, you can have this script handy and you could check that. OK, so you kind of already see me do this and I've kind of already gone over it. But, you know, if you want to just go over really quickly individually, if you want to execute any script the same as a file, you're going to want to go to, you know, the directors and it's time to send in the script name and then just hit enter. And you're going to be good to go. See, you've already seen me do that many times. And if you're going along with me, you've probably known as well. So you know how to write and execute scripts now. So we've got all of the bases and Linux bash in Python. So what's next? So now that we, you know, have some of those important, you know, scripting basics down and the bases down, we're going to quickly go over how you can maintain your privacy in a nice and safe way so no one can really be watching. You know, we're going to go over, you know, some applications and techniques that you can use to remain anonymous and safe on the web. So. I appreciate you for reading his chapter and I will see you guys in the next segment.

Remaining Anonymous chapter Overview

Welcome to chapter five and this chapter, we're going to go over how to hide your identity on the Web. This is a very important chapter here as well, because you want to be able to at all times not have any tracks lead back to you as far as any type of activity that you're doing, because as a ethical hacker, we want to always remain anonymous. We don't want to let people know who we are, what we're doing, our location, because we always want to be putting ourselves in the mind of the black hats. They're the ones that are actually taking all these precautions, that are doing all these different things to remain anonymous. And so we want to also follow in their footsteps so we can step into that frame. Right. Step into that mindset. But also understanding that when we're doing different types of testing, when we're trying out different strategies, different methods, we always, always want to be covering our tracks. And so let's go ahead and jump into the chapter five overview. In this chapter five, we're going to go over a few ways that you can hide your identity and maintain your privacy.

And specifically, what we're going to cover here is privacy. And knowing your I.P. address, this is very important here. What exactly is privacy? How does it work in the importance of knowing your IP address and how you're able to get detected through your IP address? This is something that essentially lets people know your location, your device, and it's something that you want to make sure that you are aware of at all times. Right, as far as your IP address on your device. And then we're going to go over the Tor browser. This is a browser specifically set up to be able to hide your identity. And then we're also going to go over the ANANA surf and then using a VPN where we're going to be able to set up a virtual private network and be able to connect through that so we can access different websites, different information.

So we're essentially hiding all of our traps. And then we're going to go over understanding public Wi-Fi versus home Wi-Fi and then a virtual private server recommendation from Digital Ocean for about six dollars a month. Very inexpensive. So why is it important here, first and foremost, to remain private on the Web? If you think about it, privacy can be defined as a state or condition of being free from being observed or disturbed by other people. So you are essentially hiding all information about you. You can be essentially in a whole nother country, right. In a whole different continent, and then have a specific IP address that says that you are in the states. Right. So for our purposes, for what we're doing for ethical hacking practices, we want and prefer for people not to be able to know what we're doing and know who we are, where we're located. Right.

We can be in a different continent, different country, but we want to be able to change that information so we're not able to be identified. Right. Completely remaining anonymous. And like I mentioned previously, we're wanting to mimic exactly what an actual black hacker would be doing. Right, so that we can find different loopholes that they would be able to exploit. Right. And be able to cover those, because that's essentially what an ethical hacker is. We are essentially looking at things from the perspective of a black hacker and how they would go about exploiting different loopholes so we can cover those and patch any of those books. And so a quick disclaimer here. Anything that you learn from this chapter or really any chapter within this Book is purely for educational purposes and is meant to be used for ethical hacking only. Right.

We do not advocate or approve anyone using these techniques to perform any type of malicious attacks against any device or network unless given permission to do so prior. OK, so finding your IP address, a quick and easy way to find your public IP address is to literally go to Google and type in what's my IP or my IP address. And it's going to pull that up very quickly, very easily for you to be able to see. So all you gotta do is literally go to Google, type in what's my IP? You're going to have a bunch of different search results there. Click on any one of those. It's going to tell you your IP address. And I will also tell you your location there. And just a quick explanation of your IP address. Your IP address is just like a phone number and it's specific to your particular device. So now let's go over what a sample VPN tunnel looks like. So when we're looking to remain anonymous on the Web, one of the tools that we're going to use is a virtual private network.

And what this does is it adds extra security and privacy to private and public networks. For example, if we're looking to connect a computer to a specific network and we don't want to give our IP address right on a remote computer, you'll see through this image that we will have a remote computer or our computer. Right. That goes and connects to a VPN. And so what that does now is it changes. Our IP address, our location, and it doesn't give out any of our initial computer's information or IP address, it automatically changes it. If our IP address on a remote computer is one, two, three, four, five, just an example. Then when we go to the VPN, it's maybe going to be, you know, five, eight, nine and seven, whatever. There's obviously more numbers than that in the IP address. I'm just giving you an example of how it actually changes your IP address.

And as previously mentioned, you can be in a whole different country, a whole different city, and you can get into a VPN and it'll completely change your location, your IP address. So you're completely remaining anonymous. So this is a quick chapter overview here of what's to come. We're going to dive deeper into the VPN, several different ways that you can remain anonymous through the different browsers in a bunch of other techniques and methods that you can use to achieve a completely Hijrah identity and remain anonymous on the Web. So that's going to be here for this one. And we'll see you on the next one.

TOR Browser Overview

One thing that's very, very useful when you're an ethical hacker and you want to maintain your privacy or if you just like, if you're someone that just, you know, wants to remain anonymous on the web for whatever reason, there are a lot of people that are actually very paranoid about this kind of stuff. You know, like maybe somebody's watching, maybe the government is watching, maybe they are all. So you don't necessarily want them to know, you know, what you're exactly doing. That doesn't mean that you're doing bad things. You just want to maintain your privacy. Which is it? Right. So the Tor browser is a Web browser that allows users to browse the web while preventing surveillance and tracking. Now, this is achieved by rerouting all of your requests through three other nodes, which are just other computers in the Tor ecosystem. And you prewash them as proxies. Think of it this way.

So traffic is coming from your peers, from your router, and it's going out to the Web, but it's going through three other computers. And each time, you know, it's encrypted, each time it goes through another computer. So no one, no one is going to be able to decrypt this traffic. And then, number two, you're going to have a different identity when you're on the Web. This is very, very useful. And you're going to see that, you know, your security and privacy improves drastically, you know, if you were to use the term browser. So if you want to download this on our virtual machine, we could just do a simple install of TOR and then go toward the browser launcher and we can go ahead and try that out and see if we can get Tor on our copy machine. OK, guys, so we're back at our calling machine.

So what we need to do really quickly before we can install TOR is actually update the repositories that are calisthenics, machines actually pulling updates and install requests from. So what we're going to do is we slash ATC, slash ABC slash sources list and you're going to want to add this line right here. So pause the chapter and type this line exactly as you see it right here inside of this file. And then you're going to want to do it right . Or just a quit go for me, didn't do anything, and then now if you do a pseudo Apte Dash gets updated, it should actually be able to all you know, from the repository, you know, all the different files that it needs. And then if this works right here, you should be able to update, you know, all the things on Linux, but you should also be able to go through and actually do the ABG command to install TOR so you can go ahead of your system, if you like to. If you do have an issue and it actually isn't finding or still another command that may help you may or may not have to do this.

So the ABC dash key space ATV space that says key server is KP calling for this for as long as he's G and you p g dot net and then just put dash dash i c v dash. His inner self is going to ask you this command and this is just going to go through and allow us to be able to actually pull, you know, fondness for pastoralists. If you're having an issue, you may or may not have to do that one. So after that, you've got to update and see if it works. And if it did, you're going to be good to go. So what we can do now is pseudo Apte Dash Daggett's install Tor and then we're going to do Tor browser dash launcher and now it's going to pull from online. Ask if we want to continue. Yes. So now you type in capital y enter and now it's going to go through and actually download Tor from us. And then once that, once that's done we're going to be able to, you know, go ahead and launch tours. And once this is done, we're going to check back in. I'm going to teach you guys how to launch it. OK guys, so we have to finish my install.

So now let's go ahead and use the Tor browser launcher, the launcher. And what is it going to do since it is the first time you're doing it has to download some files that go ahead and get you set up. But once this is done, it's going to open up the Tor browser for us. So let's just give it a minute. It's installed in the application. OK, so once it's installed Tor browser launch, so as you can see, it opened up this window by itself. So what you are going to want to do is if you want to configure some settings, you can, but you say connect and then it's connecting this to the torch relay and it's going to encrypt all of our communications online and routing through all the different nodes that have said that. I explained before and we're pretty much good to go. You'll be browsing anonymously, not anonymously through Tor. It may be a little bit slower than you know if you're browsing in just a regular browser. That's just because of all the, you know, extra encryption and traveling that our data has to do when we're using TOR. But it's definitely worth the privacy.

Anonsurf Overview

OK, so another option for, you know, maintaining your privacy online is to use a non serve, a non serve is a tool that's going to allow you to stay anonymous by routing, you know, every packet from your computer through the torch relay. So when you use an answer for ethical hacking, all the traffic from your system is going to go through a tour proxy server. So it's kind of similar in Tor Tor browser, but it's actually, you know, for things like when you're not in the browser, so you're doing stuff like maybe the phone command line is something that just all of the traffic is going to go through a torch relay. So if you want to download and launch for Linux, you can do the following commands so you can have the Cloney from GitHub. This is something that, you know, an ethical hacking community.

GitHub is very widely used where people postcode publicly for you to download. And one way that you can download is a git clone command, followed by the link to the actual, you know, GitHub repository that you want to clone or, you know, copy down to your computer. So it's just going to copy the folder from this location and all the files inside of it to your local computer. And you don't want to change the change to the folder called Caleigh Dash and serve and then run the installer files just to show the file and then just announce that unassertive start and then we're good to go. So let's go ahead and try this out. OK, so we're back on the calisthenics machine. So let's try this right here in California. So let's see. Get clone htp us. Let's get Hubb dot com slash undie three. Are F 10 W.

Slash Kelly Dash Anon's surf surf dive, yet the SO now was going through Cloney eight when it found all the objects, it copied it down knock and KDDI to the colonizer folder.

And then I can do, I'm going to do a pseudo just to be safe to avoid potential issues and a solid show and now it's going to go ahead and install a non-surf and once this is done we're going to be able to launch. It will just be an awesome start and then all of our pacas will be routed through Tor relays. So let's give it a minute and then we'll start it up. OK, so now we see that the installation is finished and actually launched. It's a non surf start. Make sure that you run as Ruzzo pseudo announcer starts. And then it's going to go ahead and start a tour, and now all of our traffic is being routed through tor relay, so technically we know where we're going to maintain our privacy here. So this is another option for you if you don't want to, you know, necessarily just use it in our browser if you're going to be doing other things. This is just to give you an extra layer of privacy and security.

Changing Mac Addresses

OK, so to go a little bit deeper with the privacy, there's something called Mac Changers, so every device has a unique Mac address that can be identified. And in order to remain anonymous, you know, it would be wise to change this as well because they can't be linked back to you based on a Mac address. So you have to be careful. And there's something called Mac changer that can do this for us. So if you want to install it, run it, just run the following command in the terminal. So it's going to be pseudo-everything, install Mac changer and then we're going to actually run the application after it is installed and we'll give it the interface name as an argument. So I'm going to show you that in a minute. But here's what that means. Think of it as like your Ethernet port on your computer, like, you know, a network interface right there. So we're going to change the Mac address for that specifically. That's just an example of exactly what we're about to do. But we're going to change the managers for our interface that we're using to get to the Internet. So let's go ahead and check this out.

OK, so we're back in our Caledonius machine, so let's go and do our computer to install a pseudo A.B.C. install Mac changer. So now it's going to reach out to the repositories. OK, so we're good to go. It's already started here. So let's do a Souto Mac changer. Well, first we need to figure out our interface name. So our interface that we're using to get to the Internet is this one right here is this 10 zero two down one five and the Ethernet. Eight zero is the name of the interface, so what we're going to do is we're going to run pseudo Mac changer Dash R zero. So what you're going to see is that the Mac address for this interface is going to change. So it says the current Mac right there and spits it out. And then now it's going to show us our new one right there at the bottom. So a change is successfully changing our Mac address. So now we have an extra layer of security, you know. OK, so it actually does find some way to actually look at our traffic or figure out where something is coming from. This Mac address, this Big Mac address is going to put them in the wrong direction. So more privacy for us.

Using a Virtual Private Network/Server (VPN, VPS)

OK, so another step that you can take to further hide your identity on the Internet is using VPN. So VPN permits all your traffic through an encrypted tunnel just so that you know, no one else can access your data or read your traffic or anything while you're on the web. So it's going to allow you to browse the Internet security so you can pay for a solution, use a free one online or set up your own open VPN server, unlike in the US or a digital ocean, you know, private server for about one to six dollars a month. And there's a guy right here that you guys can follow that I've used before and a chapter on, you know, doing as soon as well because I did run into some troubles and some things didn't work and figured that also there will be a chapter on assoon. So I recommend that you spin up like eight of us, a fruitier machine. It'll be free or they don't cost like six cents a month and just install the VPN server on it and then you can use that as your VPN. One was that we were taking multiple steps, this cybersecurity where you and you want to take multiple steps, multiple layers of defense. So a virtual private server.

So if you want to really keep yourself anonymous, you know, it's not required. You could set up a virtual private server. Now, this is a server that you would connect to and then execute all the commands, things like, for example, you would maybe, you know, S.H. into a virtual private server that you set up, maybe in a digital ocean and maybe eight of us. And then you could do all of your, you know, ethical hacking activities through that address. And you can implement all the other stuff that we talked about before, like a non serve, maybe the Tor browser vs the VPN, if you want to, to further, you know, provide yourself with more privacy and to keep you anonymous on the web. So when you do this, I want you to realize that none of the commands are coming from your computer. So you're going to be as anonymous as possible and you get a virtual private server or an ocean for about five dollars a month. I do that myself. I have a server within. I'm probably going to have more servers with them.

And then also eight of us is another cheap option to just spin up a virtual private server that you can use to do different things with. So we're getting very, very, very secure and anonymous. So public wi fi versus private wifi. OK, so while you might be using TOR or not serve and your IP address is changed, your Mac address is changed. There is still some small, slight potential, very, very small, but slightly possible that your traffic can be traced back to you. OK, so if you're using private Wi-Fi at your home, you could potentially be easily identified. So you want to make sure that you take the extra precautions so that you're safe. So if you really, really wanted to, you might not see this as something that you're going to need to do, you know, when you're actually going about your ethical hacking activities, but you really want to stay anonymous. You can really just go use public wi fi for all of your hacking activities.

And pretty much nothing is going to be able to be traced back to you at all. Think about it. We changed our Mac address. We're going to be using an answer. We might be using a virtual server. You might be on a VPN, you might be using the Tor browser, and then you might be on public Wi-Fi. No one is going to be able to find you can almost guarantee that I'm not going to say 100 percent, but close to it. All right. So. That's so we know how to stay anonymous now on the Web and maintain our privacy. So what's next? So we're going to start hacking now. So we're going to go over some methods. First of all, wifi hacking. Something is very interesting and very fun and something that you can actually practice at your home. All right. So we're going to practice hacking into an Internet network at your house. And also that is something that you can take into the real world as well if you're doing an actual on site, you know, penetration test or something. So I appreciate you guys. We'll listen in as far as I see you guys in the next chapter.

WiFi Hacking chapter Overview

Welcome to chapter six in this chapter, we're going to cover wifi hacking. I'm going to walk you through a big picture overview of what exactly wi fi is and how this is one of the most common ways that black hunters get access to networks, access to information, and how you can also learn how to hack wifi yourself. Right. So let's go right ahead and jump in here. So we're going to go over specifically what is Wi-Fi? I want you to get a real understanding foundationally of what exactly Wi-Fi is. Right. We have that acronym there, but we don't really know how it works, why it works and the backstory of it. Right. We're going to go into that. We're going to go over how hackers break into Wi-Fi, what are the most common methods. And then we're going to go over setting up a Calli machine for Wi-Fi hacking. We're going to walk through the hacking. We're also going to walk through the WPA and WP to hack as well.

So what exactly is Wi-Fi? So Wi-Fi is a wireless networking technology that allows devices such as computers, laptops, desktops, and any other mobile devices to interface with the Internet. So if you look at the right hand side over here, you notice that you have all these devices, right? You have the computers, you have your cell phone, you have a laptop. They're all connected to a wireless access point. Right. Which is typically like a modem that also serves as a Wi-Fi connection, which is a wireless access point that allows devices such as your cell phone. If you're walking around at home. Right. You don't need to connect your cell phone through a wired cable. Right to your modem. All you gotta do is sign up to the Wi-Fi and you'll have instant access to that network. That wireless access point serves as the actual Wi-Fi connection for any other devices in the network.

So just think about a wireless access point as the same thing as an amplifier and what an amplifier does for a home stereo. It amplifies the connection and amplifies the sound. And so an access point takes the bandwidth coming from a router and stretches it out so that more devices can get on the network. And sometimes you'll just have a wireless access point that is connected to a router. Right. You have an actual router that you can have for an actual access device. And sometimes you have a standalone wireless access point. Right. That will allow the network to stretch its actual coverage. And so this is essentially what Wi-Fi is, right? It's a wireless network, technology allowing devices to be connected to the Internet through the network on a wireless basis. And so now let's go over how hackers break into Wi-Fi. So here are some of the common methods that they use to break into the actual Wi-Fi networks. So we have been sniffing here.

And what snipping is, it allows hackers to hijack any packet of data that is being transmitted between a device and a router. So in between that connection, right. There's packets of information that are going back and forth and the hacker is able to hijack any of those bits and pieces of information while they're being transmitted. And then we have spoofing. And how this works here is, you know, typically when you log into a specific network, wireless network, you have your saved login information as far as your username and your password. And so what a black header does here is they set up a network that is stronger and that allows your particular device to connect to whatever saved information there. As far as the login, the password. Right. The credentials then get saved. And so then that information is now available to that, you know, Blackadder and then they're able to actually get the login information to the actual network that you're looking to actually connect to. And then there's word driving.

This is where hackers are physically driving around in their car and they're spotting and looking to exploit wireless local area networks while they're driving around. And this is typically for like, you know, businesses that have networks that, you know, expand to a given location in a given area. These are folks that are actually driving around looking to exploit these types of networks. And then we have encryption hacking. This is where hackers use brute force on the router in a bid to crack its decryption key. And then finally, here we have brute force. I really want to give you a full explanation here. What brute force is this is the equivalent of trying every single key on the key ring and eventually finding the right one. So let's say you have a set of numbers that you're working with. One through 10 brute force is essentially where you're going through each and every single combination within that one through 10.

Right. You're trying one trying to three to know all the numbers and you're essentially putting in all your force, all your capabilities to be able to take over that particular network. Or to get into that particular information, whatever that may be, it's doing it by all means necessary, essentially, or trying everything in the book, throwing everything at everything in the kitchen sink to essentially be able to break into that network or whatever data or application that you're breaking into. And so this is a quick chapter overview here of wifi hacking. We're going to go a lot more in-depth in these coming chapters. Anthony is going to walk you through a lot more examples, but this is more just a quick overview of understanding at a foundational level, wi fi is and what are some of the common methods that hackers use to break into wifi? So that's going to be here for this one. And we'll see you on the next one.

WiFi Hacking System Setup

So how do we get set up for this type of hacking, so in order to detect and connect to wi fi networks with our virtual machine or a Linux machine, we're going to need to use an external USB Wi-Fi adapter. The one that's in your laptop is most likely not going to work. So what you're going to need to do is actually go ahead and purchase a USB wi fi adapter if you check out the resources chapter here. And also I'll have it attached in the building at your lab chapter. I'm going to give you a recommended USB adapter, the one that I'm using so that you can go ahead and get that and then you'll be good to go. So assuming that you have the recommended adapter, you're going to need to download a virtual box extension pack so that we can actually use it with our colonics machine. And the link to get that is right here. So I'm going to show you guys a really quick witted downloader. So you're going to want to go to this link, let the website load, and then look right here where it says Oracle VM Virtual Box Estancia.

So just download it. So click there, download it, save it is going to be this far right here. So once that's saved and on your computer, just double click it and it'll open up Oracle Box, VM Virtual Box and then is going to install it for you. So it's pretty quick and painless. So how do we attach this to our Linux machine? So you're going to want to open up the virtual box VM manager selection machine and then click on settings, go to the USB settings that you see on the left there, and then you're going to want to click the little icon. It's like it looks like a USB USB on the right side with a green plus on it. So go ahead and click that and then choose the adapter that you got and then you are just going to hit. OK, so we're going to go through this just as you guys can see how to do this. OK, so I'm in a virtual box, so I'm going to write. Click go to settings on my machine. I'm going to go over to USB and then this is already checked. It enables the plus right here.

So you see, this is my microphone. This is my wifi card that I use on my laptop. So it's just different things that are already, you know, plugged into the computer. So I don't have my Wi-Fi adapter plugged in yet. So what I'm going to do is click off this and I'm actually going to plug it in and we're going to see, you know, what changed. So let's hit it again. So now we know that this is real Tech 2.0 11 and Nikhat, that's exactly what we want. So it's there to be checked. So we're going to hit, OK? And now our colonics machine is set up to be able to use this adapter. And one other thing as well is that you guys might want to. Right. Click and go to settings and then we'll change the network's name really quickly. So we have our first adapter right here on that so that we can get to the Internet because we're going to need that.

But we're going to what we're going to want to do is actually add another adapter and choose the host only adapt adapter option right there so that we can be we can switch that out adapter into colonics machine when we need to and actually be able to connect to that private network with just a host in our VMS from Virtual Box. So once you do that, you said, OK, then we're good to go. OK, guys, so we're in our machine. So what we can do to check to make sure that it is detecting our USB adapter as we go up here to devices USB and then in this case, is the real tech able to get 11 and notecard. So this is what we want. So you want to make sure that that's checked, just confirm that. So right now, if it were going to be working correctly, when we do if config, it's just like a W lan interface. So do I have a config super secret password.

And with this with this particular adapter, you might notice that it doesn't have Dublin on theirs. That means that you have to install this driver first. So that's going to be our next step. We're going to need to install some things on our coffee machine to make sure that we can use the recommended adapter for this Book. So we have to send some commands first. The first thing you don't want to do is to install DRM systems or dynamic or modules is just going to allow us to install, you know, different kernel modules versus the regular ones on our colleague Linux machine. And then when I clone this, this repository changes to the directory and then does an install of the install file that's going to install the driver that we need for this to work. And also, if you haven't done this yet, add these two lines to your Etsy slash ABC slash sources that list files and then do an ABC update in.

Upgrade man, just to make sure that your quality distribution is up to date with all the latest modules and everything, and if you run into an error, like doing the first steps up here, like with decamps and running and stuff, I'll do this, restart your computer and then come back and then it should work for you. So I'm going to go ahead and show you guys the process of installing those things. OK, so like I said before, I already had this installed, but this is a really quick install. The cameras have already been installed. It's just going to look and try to pull it down for you to upgrade to for you to install it. Then you're going to want to clone this GitHub repository. So it's CPUs, it hub dot coms as air crack and G slash r t l eighty one to you. And it's just going to clone this repository down and copy it into the current directory. And then from there we can switch to the folder that is created and then we can go ahead and run that install file. So I already have it installed so my shoe is back in here when I do it.

But just for the sake of so you guys know how to do it, that is pseudo slash decamps in store. So is saying that for me, but it's already installed on mine, I could do pseudo decamps , I don't worry, you can do pseudo dicamba status and you can see you already have this installed. All right there, so if you get this area, I wouldn't worry about it too much, just make sure your systems are up to date and try it again and then it should at least install this. And then you're pretty much good to go at that point. So what you can do is you can click up here, make sure and you can see that it's actually picking up wireless networks now. So if I do Asuda, I have config now I can see how this plan interfaces right here. So now we're able to use our wireless adapter with our colonics machine.

OK, so there's some more steps to start to use it for our purposes and we have to put it in the monitor mode and be able to, you know, so that we're able to detect, you know, hack into Wi-Fi networks. We have to put it into this monitoring mode and allow us to detect networks that are in range and sniff the traffic. The Wi-Fi adapter, you know, should be managed by the fall. So we have to change just by executing a few commands. We have to turn the interface off and then use air mining and kill it. And then we're going to do RW config and change their mind and change it to remote and then bring the interface back up. So let's go do that really quickly. Go back on the Linux machines. What we're going to do is we're going to do our config to zero down. This is going to put the wireless LAN interface down and then we're going to do air mine and G check kill and this is going to go through and kill the networking services pretty much, and it'll stay off until you turn it back on. We'll talk about that after that.

I started to do his thing and then when I do, I can feed the villain zero. Mode monitor, and this is going to put it into monitoring mode and then we're going to bring the interface back with I have config that we land zero up. So now if you do what I have configured, you see we have willand zero. And when you look at it now. When you see this here, this indicates, you know, we know that it's in monitoring mode, so now we can use this to attack and hack into networks. One thing to know, you may have to restart the networking services because this actually, you know, kills the network manager. So you're not going to have access to the Internet. We do this. So use the service network manager start. But we don't really need that, you know, for our wifi hacking purposes.

WEP Hacking Attack #1

OK, so before we actually learn to crack into it well, try to understand it and its weaknesses just a little bit more so WEAP is pretty old. It dates back to 1997 when Wi-Fi was first introduced to the world. I was five years old a long time ago. The main floor, though, with WEAP was using small IVs, and the size of the encryption key, which was pretty small, was either 64 bit or 128 bit. So in the IVs they make up twenty four bits of the encryption key and they were used along with the secret key to encrypt with the C4 cipher. So each packet is supposed to have a different I.V. but due to its size, reuse is very common, like on a busy network. So since the IVs are only twenty four bits long and the rest of the key is always the same, the total number of combinations are very small and pretty easy, you guys.

So at the RC four cipher screens for a given IV are actually found. An attacker can decrypt packets that are sent that were encrypted with the same IV and we can forge packets. So this means that you don't really need to know the Webbe to decrypt packets if you know what key string was used to encrypt that packet. So, you know, technically you are doing it manually. I know it sounds a little bit complicated. It's got a high level of how it works. But we have tools that can do this automatically and literally in a matter of minutes or maybe even seconds, we're going to be using called aircraft. And so it is primarily used to hack into, you know, wi-fi networks. And it has a whole suite of different tools that we're going to be using that's going to help us attack, you know, web networks and also networks later on.

So the first attack that we're going to do is actually, you know, capturing packets and then we're going to crack the key using those packets is basically what we said before. So we're going to use an arrow up M.G., part of the aircraft and G suite to capture a large number of packets flowing over a network, you know, into a file. And then we're going to use that file to actually crack the Wep key, you know, with air cracking. So now let's go over to our scene, actually try to do this attack. OK, so back on Callaghan's machine. So I went and changed my router settings. I turned. So for WEAP, I had to go down to a two point four megahertz frequency for it in order to enable the weapon. I put it like a password in areas like Hack Me Please with ease on it and try to fit like all the characters. It's like a certain character requirement for how to do that.

So now we're going to try to see if we can find the network with our wireless card. So let's check to make sure we have config. OK, we still have a Wlan device there and it is running in monitoring mode. So we're going to do our first command. So we're going to try to capture all the two point four gigahertz networks. So that's the arrow dump and G and then Dash Dash band and we're going to be and then put Queenland zero because that's the interface that we're going to be using. And B represents two point five gigahertz frequency and then we're going to go ahead and enter. We have to be Souto. So actually one way to avoid having to do pseudo autonomous or pseudo high command and you become a route. So now we can try to stay in command without having to do that.

It's kind of annoying anyway. So that says Band B between zero and then now is capturing all the networks that are in two point four gigahertz. And now what you want to do is actually look for the one that is for your network, so mine is probably the one right here that is the only Web network. So let me expand this really quickly. So it has the names over here. So this is mine right here. OK, so what we're going to want to take note of is the B side. So for my network this is right here. So I'm going to want to copy that. And this is how this is going to allow us to actually directly target that network. So now let's see who's connected to this network. So we do Arrow, Dump and G again and then Dash, Dash B as a side. And that's just the name. It's going to be the Mac address of your router. So we're going to paste what we copied and then we're going to choose the channel. So you see the column, we need the channel numbers.

So for mine it was to do Channel 11. So it's to 11. And then, right, this does not allow us to write all the data that we're capturing into a file. So we're just going to say, Watpac, what it's going to say that and then DoubleLine zero is the interface. So this is the command. So now let's say enter and let's see what happens. So now what it is going to do is to start to capture the different devices that are actually connected to the network. So let's give it some time and we'll see, you know, exactly what devices are on this network. OK, so my laptop is the only thing that's connected there. And you can confirm that this is the address, the Mac address for your computer that you're testing like that's connected to the network. You can go do like in Windows IP fixation on look at the physical address for that adapter on this connecting to the network, and then you'll be able to see that it actually matches, sort of knows that this is this is my it sees that my laptop is connected.

OK, so for this attack, what we're going to do is so we have now this dot cap file. OK, so what we're going to do is we're going to use aircraft and G to actually try to decrypt and spit the key out. So let's do air, crack, dash and G and then the file names of Watpac zero one cat. And then we're going to enter and now are going through and are going to try to hack, so now it says I didn't have enough initialization vectors. So I'm going to go back and run the other command again. And we're going to try to write this again, and I'm going to try to get my computer to do a lot of traffic. So I'll be back and we're going to see how many different packages are captured. OK, so I have this running still capturing a lot of packets. Said about sixty thousand right there. So we can go ahead and try the aircraft and command again and see if it actually works. OK, so it actually works. So after it captured sixty thousand lives, it actually was able to crack the password. So it actually got to ask you for my right here and it also has the X format right here.

So what we can do is just to test, to make sure that actually works, that you guys don't think I'm, you know, making up. We can just copy that and what we can do. If we can try on my computer, so let's go, let's disconnect. OK, so it asked me to enter the network, so I actually put it in there. So let's see, it's going to be hack me, please, to ease on the air and just see you guys can see. How can we please? Next, verifying and connecting. And we should be able to successfully connect to this network, so it's saying that it isn't secure. This is like a windows, I guess, security feature in some way. It doesn't stop you from connecting those still connecting. And now we have a. Successful Internet connection. It is connected, so we're good to go. We learned how to crack wep encryption and this was the highest level with the 128 bit key. So it was still able to crack, you know, in a short amount of time. It only took, what, six seconds? OK, so that's pretty cool. So now what we can do is move on to try some other types of attacks.

WEP Hacking Attack #2

OK, so now we can move on to another attack, it's going to be fake authentication replay. So this is something that we can do if you're having trouble, like having a lot of data on your network so they can capture a lot of Evy's you can try this attack out. So we're going to use erodible energy to capture the package into a file once again. And then we're going to use er er replay Engie to perform a fake authentication attack to associate, you know, with the Target network or a.k.a. your router and you know, allow us to force the right to create more Ivey's and then we're going to increase the network activity with our . So after that we can use the aircraft engine to actually crack the key, just like the first attack first. And now we're going to do this attack if we're actually going to do the fake authentication to actually associate with the network.

So let's go ahead and let's run. And again, just like we did before Aradigm and Jegan, and then we're going to write into a file called Fake Up, and now it's going to pick up the different devices that are connected to the network, as you know. So now it's like doing a fake association with it. So this command right here, every play dashed as fake. All this means is doing a fake authentication attack and zero just means to do it once. And then we have Dash A and then this is the Mac address of the network, which we already know where to find that. And that's H. This is the Mac address of our wireless adapter that we have connected to colonics. And you could find that by going over and doing an ISP and then looking at these first 12 digits right here and changing the hyphens to Colon's, and that is the Mac address of our wireless adapter that we have connected.

So what we can do is go back over here and now and then you also have to put the interface, which is zero, and then you're going to hit enter and it is going to associate us. OK, so now if we check back over here, we can see that right here. This is the device where we did the fake authentication. It's like this is the Mac and just my wireless adapter. And you can see that we're associated underoath right here. It was blank before, but now this is open. Just another way to see that we've actually successfully associated with this and now we're going to try the replay attack. So it's a very similar command. You want to change the Dash eight, it should be right here and then change the fake all to our replay once you take out the zero as well. Don't need that there.

And then we're just going to enter and now it's just going to kind of send a bunch of packets to the router. And now we're going to see that the packets everything's, you know, kind of increasing very, very quickly. The frames are going up and the day being captured is going up a little bit faster than before. So what you want to do is a way that you can kind of speed up the capture of packets on this network just in case, you know, you have a kind of slow network. And it's just another way to gather more Ivey's so that you can go ahead and crack the network. So you want to let you give a little bit of time and then you can try to air and command again and you'll be good to go. OK, so if you notice that the data and the data number is going up really slow, what you can do is actually go over and try to do another fake authentication attack just so that you can be associated with the network.

And then this number should start going up very, very quickly. So once this gets a little bit higher for me, this key is about like it's 128 bits, which is the max for I probably want about thirty thousand in the data column, so I'll wait until then and then I will go ahead and try to crack it. OK, so now my package is approaching thirty thousand, so I'm going to go ahead and try it again. So let's see, let's do air crack and G and then the fake author is going to be OK this time. This is the second time I'm doing this and then we're going to, we're going to see what happens. Should actually be able to have twenty four thousand IVs. Let's see if it actually cracks. So after they captured thirty seven thousand IVs, I was able to decrypt it in less than a minute, 59 seconds. It got the same exact passes before. And we know that I showed you before. So now you know, you know how to crack into networks. And now we're going to move on to doing networks, which is a little bit more a little different of an approach.

What Next

So now that we know how to crack into the web now, let's go over how to crack the WPA and most likely what you're going to see, you know, out in the real world. So, you know, once we get, you know, obviously became, you know, an issue and it was easy to hack and everybody was doing it. They made WPA and WPA to, you know, as the replacements. So they use very strong encryption methods. And, you know, they're not really hackable by the same method as we did with each packet, with the WPA and is encrypted with a temporary key. So that prediction, like with the Ives and Webb of Webb, makes it almost impossible. So the best method of actually trying to hack into WPA and the WPA practically is to capture the four way handshake.

So whenever you try to connect to a Wi-Fi network that's using WPA and WPA two, there's a four way hand that kind of happens as you authenticate and and like like we first connect and try to authenticate to the access point and this package that is sent back and forth, we can use what's in those packets to actually figure out, you know, if Akeda we use, you know, is valid or if it isn't valid and can be achieved by doing a deal authentication. This acts like knocking the host off the network and then there when you knock off, when you knock them, want to know where they're going to automatically try to reconnect. And when they reconnect, we're going to capture those four way handshakes for when they try to reconnect to the network. And we're going to use Arrow Energy to actually capture that. Then we can use this. We have the handshake packets.

We can go ahead and create a wireless and then we can recover that. He can breathe pretty quickly, pretty easily. Let's go ahead and try it out. OK, so we're going to crack into a WPA or WPA so we're going to go back to our calisthenics machine and we're going to run an arrow up again. So what I'm doing here, I have the best idea, the physical Mac address of the router that I'm trying to get into, put the channel that is specifically on and I'm writing everything that is capturing to a file called Aperture Handshake is going to go to the current folder that we're in. And then I'm also specifying the band. I found that if I didn't do that, I would have some issues. So you could do that, if you like. And then I put in my wireless interface, which is Dublin zero, and then we just run that. And now it's going to start to pick up the devices as we've seen before. So you can see up here, that's actually true. Now for authentication.

Hospice care. Appreciate Shirkey. So now it's picking up the different devices that are actually connected to this access point. So what we can do is we can run the authentication attack for the wireless card I'm using for my computer. And it's currently connected. It has a sort of there, but it's currently connected. And I know that this is the Mac address for that. So we're going to do every play and this dash zero followed by a space in a zero is a dual authentication, in fact, is going to send an infinite number of packets. And so we actually tell it to stop and then dash a right. Here is the Mac address of the router and then Dachsie is the Mac address of the client or their target computer or, you know, my wireless. And after that I connected and I had issues. If I didn't put this dash in there, it's going to be much like force the attack force in the packets.

So if you run into issues where it says, you know, no such business idea available, I would put that in there. And then the wireless interface, Dublin zero, and now it's sending the authentication packets. And what I notice as well is that sometimes, you know, the computer might actually like or the wireless adapter, it might actually reconnect very quickly. So it may or may not affect the Internet connection, but it's still, you know, Cindi's authentication packets. And I believe that some of them might not actually work. But if we switch back over here, we actually see right here that we've actually caught the handshake. So what we can do now is actually create a wireless so we can actually have a lot of this since we have it. And then we can cancel all of this as well, because we have the handshake and now it's captured in that file capture handshake.

So what we can do is actually create a wireless with an application called Crunch, and it's going to pretty much allow us to create a wireless that's going to let us, you know, try to pronounce brute force and figure out using this file that we captured the handshake. And we're going to use that, like we said before, against this wireless and try to figure out if, you know, one of these passwords is going to work. So I've already got a command over here. So the way that you're going to use crutches, you put Krunch in the. This first number right here is the minimum number of characters, so I'm putting nine and then the maximum number of characters is nine. So it's going to make passwords that only have nine nine characters. Do you know, like six to like 10 if you wanted to, in case you didn't exactly know? I know exactly.

And just to save time and effort with this, I put the password to this right here, just just so that you guys can see, you know, the capabilities of this. And so what you can do is you would put like, you know, after these numbers, you'll put what characters you want to be included in the password. So it can be like, you know, one, two, three, four, eight, Afgooye. It'll only include these letters when it's making the password. So every combination of these letters in there and then the Dashty option right here allows you to do a pattern. So if I wanted the password to always start with 56 and then have maybe, you know, so one, two, three, four. So these symbols right here actually indicate, you know, fill it with any of the other any of the available characters, and then you can then you can finish like maybe it always ends with, you know, seven, six, seven, eight, you know. And so what we'll do is it will make a pass, but it starts with five, six. It fills in these with the different character options that you gave it.

And then it always ends with six, seven, eight so low it drastically lowers like the number of, you know, possible passwords, so or words. So let me actually show you an example. For our specific example, I already set the password. So we're going to say word lists of nine with nine characters in them, and then we're going to set the password to this. So it's going to make every combination of these letters. And then if we were to do that, it's a really big file as three gigabytes. So what we can do is we can refine this using the debt, the option, and then we can, you know, set it, give it a pattern. So let's say like we want the patzer to always start with H and and, you know, we want anything in between this because we know it's possible to h i maybe we have a hunch we can make it fill in every single one between this using at Symbol. So we will put one, two, three, four, five, six, seven, unless we want to always end in Z.

So as you can see, this file is a lot smaller. OK, so now I am creating the world. So what you want to do is we can actually output this into a file. So be D'Ascenzo and then, you know, just worthless. So now we are going to create it and put it all, all of those into the file and then we can use that to crack into the network. So now is done and we can go ahead and try and crack G Command actually using the file that we created just now along with the cafA that we created earlier. So I see her crack dash and G and then we're going to put the name of the cat, the cat file which was the capture. Handshake. Yep. Cap. And then we're going to put Dash W and then put our file that we just created where it lists and then enter and now er crack is going to run.

So it says take a while because it's a pretty big list. So you might want to try to refine the list a little bit more. So what we can do, we can actually. Go back and refine this a little bit more. So let's say that just to save us time so we know that it starts with a pack. So we can all put this into where this is probably going to overwrite the file. So now there is only six thousand five hundred sixty one line, so now it is done. So let's go ahead and try air cracking again. And to take a lot less time and is going to find it, he found, hack me, please. So that actually works. So now. We know that the password for this network is actually how we please and we use the file that we captured from Arrow Dump, you know, to actually go through and verify it with aircraft. So now you know how to hack into people's Wi-Fi.

Don't use this maliciously, please. Now you guys know how to crack into , how to crack and then to utilize the powerful stuff. So now that we know how to do that, you know what's next. So we're going to actually go about actually, you know, when you connect to a network, you know how to discover more information about the devices and actually find vulnerabilities. So we're going to use a variety of tools to do that. But I'm going to teach them different techniques using open source intelligence as well, so that you guys can learn how to gather information for an attack. Like maybe you're doing a penetration test in the future. You're going to know exactly how to gather information. So I appreciate you for listening as far as the next book.

www.ingramcontent.com/pod-product-compliance
Lightning Source LLC
Chambersburg PA
CBHW071925210526
45479CB00002B/556